Machine Guns
and the
Great War

Machine Guns and the Great War

Paul Cornish

Pen & Sword
MILITARY

First published in Great Britain in 2009
And reprinted in this format in 2021 by
PEN AND SWORD MILITARY
an imprint of Pen & Sword Books Ltd,
47 Church Street, Barnsley, S. Yorkshire, S70 2AS

ISBN: 978-1-39901-451-9

For more information on our books, please visit
www.frontline-books.com, email info@frontline-books.com
or write to us at the above address.

Printed and bound by CPI Group (UK) Ltd, Croydon, CR0 4YY
Typeset by Concept, Huddersfield, West Yorkshire

Pen & Sword Books Ltd incorporates the imprints of Pen & Sword
Archaeology, Atlas, Aviation, Battleground, Discovery,
Family History, History, Maritime, Military, Naval, Politics,
Social History, Transport, True Crime, Claymore Press,
Frontline Books, Praetorian Press,
Seaforth Publishing and White Owl

For a complete list of Pen and Sword titles please contact
PEN & SWORD LTD
47 Church Street, Barnsley, South Yorkshire, S70 2AS, England
E-mail: enquiries@pen-and-sword.co.uk

Or

PEN AND SWORD BOOKS
1950 Lawrence Rd, Havertown, PA 19083, USA
E-mail: Uspen-and-sword@casematepublishers.com

To H J W

Contents

List of Plates

right is using a Barr and Stroud rangefinder, which was also used in conjunction with the Vickers gun.

17. A French CSRG gunner of the 53rd Colonial Infantry Regiment. The distinctive pouches on his belt each contain two magazines. He also carries a 7.65mm pistol purchased from Spain: standard issue for CSRG gunners.

18. An abandoned German machine gun nest. The MG08 is mounted on a simple trench-mount, of the type favoured for forward machine gun positions. The gun's former owners have disabled it by removing the feed block.

19. German prisoners. The man at the rear is shouldering an MG08/15 light machine gun.

20. German machine guns captured by the British. A captured Russian M1905 Maxim gun and a Madsen *Muskete*.

21. The Villar Perosa gun, here used as originally envisaged – with a heavy armoured shield.

22. The Austrian M12/P16 machine pistol, minus its detachable stock.

23. A diagram showing the machine gun scheme for II Anzac Corps at the Battle of Messines. The shaded areas were intended to receive standing barrages. The ladder-like successions of lines indicate creeping barrages.

24. Lieutenant Val Browning with his father's M1917 machine gun.

25. John M. Browning (left), the inventor of the M1918 automatic rifle, examines an early example of the weapon with Mr Burton, the Winchester expert on rifles.

26. General Odlum and other officers of 11th Canadian Brigade inspect a captured MP18 machine pistol.

27. An armoured 'Autocar' truck of the Canadian Motor Machine Gun Brigade going into action at the Battle of Amiens, 9 August 1918.

28. French and British troops with a Model 1914 Hotchkiss machine gun, during the retreat of 1918. The arrival of the enemy is evidently not imminent as the gun is not loaded and one of its crew is enjoying a pipe.

29. The machine gun war as imagined by *The War Illustrated*, 1916. British troops burst into a strongpoint occupied by cowering German machine-gunners.

Acknowledgements

I have chosen to dedicate this book to the memory of the late Herbie Woodend, former Custodian of the MoD Pattern Room. There will, I suppose, come a day when writers of books relating to firearms can dispense with acknowledging the influence of that remarkable man; but the time is not yet come. This book certainly owes much to the fact that some of his enthusiasm for firearms, along with a tiny scrap of his unrivalled knowledge of the subject, appears to have rubbed off on me. I am similarly indebted to Dolf Goldsmith, machine gun historian and machine-gunner, with whom I have spent instructive hours among the machine guns. These were the men who, between them, inspired me to embark on the study of the technology and its application.

With regard to the historical perspective, it was Professor Peter Simkins who, in 1997, first prompted me to investigate the doings of British machine-gunners during the First World War. As to the actual writing of this work, I am greatly indebted to Chris McCarthy for reading each chapter as it was written. Not only did he helpfully point out my errors, and suggest structural changes that have greatly improved the finished product but, also, most importantly for me, encouraged me to believe that my conclusions held water.

For the material culture aspects of this book, I must first of all thank Dr Nick Saunders for opening my eyes to this discipline and its possibilities. I should also add my apologies for the fact that these matters occupy a somewhat subordinate position in the book. There was just too much history to cram in. Further thanks for assistance with this element of the book must go to Professor Paul Gough.

The following colleagues are also due a vote of thanks for their generosity with time and information: Alan Jeffreys and Vicky Wylde of the Imperial War Museum, Richard Jones of the National Firearms Centre, and Dominiek Dendooven of the In Flanders Fields Museum at Ieper.

Finally thanks to my partner Kim and son Thomas – temporary machine gun widow and orphan respectively – for their support, practical input and making a damned good pretence of not being bored stiff.

Prologue

Taking Aim

Of the deadly work beneath that pall of smoke, as steel met steel and the new soldiers of Britain fleshed their bayonets for the first time, and fell by the thousand under the murderous fire of machine-guns, history will tell the tale long after the survivors have ceased to recount the deeds of the day to their grandchildren wherever the English tongue is spoken.

(Thomas Russell, *America's War for Humanity*)

At 7.30 am on 1 July 1916 eleven divisions of the British Expeditionary Force commenced the offensive officially known as the Battle of Albert – in an action which has become better known to posterity as the 'First Day of the Somme'. By the end of the day the attackers had sustained 57,470 casualties – including 19,240 killed. These were, and remain, the highest casualties ever suffered by the British Army in the course of a single day. The events of this momentous day have been chronicled and analysed exhaustively by British historians. Indeed further discussion of the disaster here might be seen as superfluous. However, the impact made by the events of 1 July 1916 is of central importance to the subject of this book: for it was the machine gun which dominated the recollections of those who survived that day, and which has become emblematic of both this battle and, by extension, of the Great War as a whole.

Certainly the first day of the Somme witnessed what was probably the zenith of the machine gun's use as a direct fire weapon. A German analysis of the day, based on interviews with wounded British prisoners, concluded that machine guns were:

beyond doubt the main strength of the German defence, against which the attackers stood 'no chance', as they called it. The destructive power of the machine gun is the cause of the enormous losses they sustained, and the first impetus of the attack was on many occasions broken just by the fire of the machine guns in the first German line. The machine-gunners were magnificent, and so was the way their weapons were sited. All the prisoners, including the officers, are unanimous on that point.[1]

The very topography of the Somme battlefield aided the German defenders, who made skilled use of high ground and the numerous folds, valleys and re-entrants in siting their machine guns. Their intention, in which they were largely successful, was to maximize the possibilities for firing in enfilade (i.e. from the flank), while minimizing their exposure to British fire. The machine guns were either distributed along the German front line or grouped in the 'redoubts' (*Festen*) and fortified villages which dominated the battlefield from the high ground. Their crews were well protected; having the benefit of deep dugouts carved into the accommodating chalk of the Somme plateau. Their firing positions were generally reinforced with concrete and steel.

It was the deep dugouts which ensured that ample numbers of machine guns and gunners survived the British bombardment. Furthermore, there proved to be sufficient time after the lifting of the bombardment for the German machine-gunners to bring up their weapons and man them before the attackers could reach their trenches. Major James Jack, preparing to attack with the 2nd Cameronians, was immediately aware of them: 'We knew at 7.30 that the assault had started through hearing the murderous rattle of German machine guns, served without a break, notwithstanding our intense bombardment, which had been expected to silence them.'[2] The popular image of the first day of the Somme pits slowly moving, heavily laden lines of British infantry against German machine-gunners who proceed to cut them down (as one German witness put it) 'like ripe corn before the scythe'. Such scenes were indeed enacted on several sectors of the 27,000-yard front, although recent research has made clear that a variety of tactical approaches were applied to the problem of traversing no man's land. Nevertheless, even single German machine guns, manned by resolute crews, were able to wreak havoc among the attackers. One of the latter, Lieutenant Dickinson of the 10th Lincolnshire Regiment recalled in an interview:

> the enfilade machine-gun fire – the air was full of bullets and the men began to fall all around us. It was tragic. When these men were hit with bullets, they just fell flat on their face and the air was full of bullets. I got one between my fingers, just clipped a bit out of each. When we came to want something to eat, when you got your haversack off your back you found that the bullets had gone through your Machonachie ration or tin of bully beef.[3]

Even where successful penetrations of the German defences were made, such as by the 36th Division around the Schwaben redoubt, further progress and the arrival of reinforcements was curtailed by the fire of unsubdued machine guns on the flanks. In the most terrible incidents, whole units were ravaged while advancing over open ground before they even reached the British start line. The most infamous example is that of the Newfoundland Regiment, which lost as many as 90 per cent of its effectives in this fashion. A similar disaster was witnessed by Major Jack, who watched as 2nd West Yorkshire Regiment attempted to advance: 'The enemy's machine guns, some 1400 yards from my position, now swept the crest like a hurricane and with such accuracy that many of the poor fellows were shot at once. This battalion had 280 casualties in traversing the 600 yards to our front line.'[4] These horrors were largely the result of well emplaced machine guns firing at considerable range – almost 2,000 metres in the case of the latter incident. The attackers found however that blasts of automatic fire could also be delivered at much shorter ranges. Prisoners related that 'The fire of the German machine guns was such that a breakthrough proved unthinkable. The German machine-gunners opened up only when the British were thirty or fifty metres from the trench under attack, and the element of surprise threw them into disorder.'[5] This sort of fire was carried out by the machine guns which were interspersed throughout the German forward defensive zone, largely mounted on extemporized mounts, which made them quick to bring into action, if unsuited for accurate long-range work. It is safe to say that, wherever and in whatever fashion the British infantryman found himself advancing on that fateful morning, there was a German machine gun waiting to greet him.

The machine gun in context

The events of 1 July 1916 are of the deepest importance to British perceptions of the Great War, and, perhaps, of war in general. As one historian has recently put it:

> At the time of writing almost a century has passed since the Battle of the Somme. That interval of time is still probably not long enough to enable us to gauge its full impact on British life.[6]

One very noticeable effect of this phenomenon is that the first day has come to represent the whole 141 days of the Somme battle in the consciousness of the public and even that of some historians. For instance, A J P Taylor's *The First World War: An Illustrated History* dismisses the events of 2 July to 18 November 1916 in a single paragraph. It is one of the ironies of First World War historiography that this highly personal, political and frequently waspish little volume should have become the most widely read history of the war. Nevertheless, the author was by no means wrong when he stated that 'The Somme set the picture by which future generations saw the First World War: brave helpless soldiers; blundering obstinate generals; nothing achieved.'

The machine gun is, of course, firmly placed at the very heart of this vision. Indeed it tends to be regarded as both the cause of trench warfare and the principal author of the Great War's hideous toll of casualties. It is my contention that this popular perception inflates the overall importance of the machine gun, while simultaneously underestimating its true potentialities. By this I mean that its role as a direct fire weapon, as exemplified by the events 1 July 1916, has elevated the machine gun to the status of an icon – a cipher for the allegedly 'futile' slaughter of the Western Front. This myth is so strong that it obscures the truth about how machine guns were actually employed and their true place in the armoury of the Great War. In the limited context of 1 July 1916, it is not difficult to see how such a misapprehension should have arisen. The 'First Day of the Somme' was however, not representative of the war as a whole.

In 1992 I was fortunate enough to meet a machine-gunner veteran of the First World War. I seem to recall that he was ninety-seven at the time. He retained a lively memory of his experiences and could still enumerate all the different potential causes of stoppages, which machine-gunners were trained to diagnose from the position of the gun's crank handle. This is not an experience I will ever have again. The generation that fought the Great War has all but departed. It should be time to view the war as history and in its true context – not through the distorting prisms of subsequent conflicts and social and political changes. Brian Bond has articulated the conviction that 'the time is now coming when the First World War can be treated as history (like earlier wars) rather than being approached emotionally and polemically in terms of "futility", "horror" and "national trauma"'.[7] The same historian's work on the historiography of the war makes it abundantly clear that the changing perception of the war since 1918 is a subject worthy of study in its own right – a fact borne out in a number of other excellent recent studies.[8] The machine gun and its use have formed an important filament of this tangled historiological growth but, strangely, have seldom been the subject of serious historical study. I hope that this book will go some way to addressing this neglect.

First of all it is worthwhile to consider the general status of the machine gun on the battlefields of the Great War. It is no secret that during the Somme battle as a whole, and indeed during the whole course of the war, the real killer was artillery. British casualty returns indicated that explosive munitions, rather than small arms fire, caused almost 60 per cent of deaths and wounds. Moreover, it was estimated that a man struck in the chest by shrapnel or a shell fragment was three times more likely to perish than a man similarly wounded by small arms fire.[9] It was primarily shellfire, not machine gun fire, which drove the armies into entrenchments and dugouts. Thereafter the situation perpetuated itself, as more and more shells were hurled in an attempt to overcome these defences. The war became an artillery war. Heavy concentrations of guns were seen as the key to breaking the trench deadlock and they did indeed frequently permit attacking troops to 'break in' to enemy positions. The disaster of the First Day of the Somme has itself been plausibly characterized as, primarily, the result of the failure of the artillery plan to live up to expectations: thus forcing the advance to take place in the face of unsuppressed defensive fire. Ironically, even when a 'break-in' was achieved, it was the subsequent difficulty in moving artillery forward that proved the principal obstacle to achieving the elusive 'breakout' (although the relatively primitive state of battlefield command, control and communications were also a major problem in this context).

The machine gun lacked both the range and the killing power of artillery. Men who kept their heads below ground level were impervious to its bullets. 'Artillery was the killer; artillery was the terrifier. Artillery followed the soldier to the rear, sought him out in his billet, found him on the march.'[10] This was borne out by the sentiments of the front-line soldiers. Machine guns did not generally feature among the perils which they most feared. Artillery bombardment, the threat of being buried alive, gas, flamethrowers and mortars appear to have been hated with equal passion by the men of all armies. Bullets, by contrast, were regarded as a relatively 'clean' way to get wounded or killed. A French infantryman summed it up thus: 'To die from a bullet seems to be nothing; parts of our being remain intact; but to be dismembered, torn to pieces, reduced to pulp, this is a fear that flesh cannot support.'[11]

I enter these caveats simply to provide a context for the remainder of the book – which of course focuses on the power and effectiveness automatic small arms.

The scope and limitations of this book

Having commenced work on this study convinced of the subordinate position of machine guns on the First World War battlefield, I have, conversely, been very forcibly persuaded of the completely dominant position which they attained among the weaponry of the infantry. Major-General J F C Fuller characterized the machine gun as 'concentrated essence of infantry'. For a man who combined the role of 'armoured warfare prophet' with excursions into the occult and Fascist politics, this is a surprisingly prosaic metaphor. However, it certainly coincides with the view prevalent in 1914. With the exception of a few radical thinkers striving to be heard from the lower depths of the officer classes, the military establishments of the pre-war era were united in regarding the

machine gun as an *augmentation of infantry firepower*. This was a very circumscribed way of thinking about the machine gun, which is in fact capable of
carrying out tasks that no number of riflemen, however highly trained, can ever
achieve. Tactics capable of exploiting the true potential of machine guns were
in their infancy in 1914. The war was to transform this situation. Furthermore,
an astonishing increase in the scale of use of automatic firepower was to take
place before the Armistice of November 1918.

Readers will be well aware that much criticism has, in the past, been directed
at military establishments that have been identified as deficient in their attitude
towards the employment of automatic firepower. This is just one element of
another popular myth of the First World War; namely that which perceives
front-line soldiers as 'victims', directed into hopeless and bloody battles by
incompetent Generals and Staff Officers. It would be superfluous for me to
reiterate here the arguments of the many works of history that have made
this simplistic version of events untenable for any open-minded student of
the subject. Suffice to say that this is another area, at least in the Anglophone
world, where myth is more tenacious than reality. Here we reach the juncture
at which historians are reluctantly obliged to admit their limitations; for their
work has had little impact on the output of journalists, television producers
and writers of fiction. Indeed, one recent study has argued persuasively that
this peculiarly British 'myth' of the First World War is even more firmly
entrenched than it ever was.[12] Consequently, I have not written this book with
the expectation or intention of changing this state of affairs. Nevertheless, its
contents will run contrary to this popular convention and, perhaps, contrary to
the expectations of even the more specialist reader.

The British military has been on the receiving end of more vitriol than most
for its apparent indifference to machine guns; either in the form of attacks
upon the War Office, or 'the Generals'. I do not wish to make this book merely
another contribution to the timeworn controversy regarding the performance
of the British Army and its commanders during the First World War. This
debate has reached such a pitch in Britain that I fear that it is sometimes in
danger of obscuring the existence of the war outside the confines of the British
Expeditionary Force's operations in France and Flanders. Nevertheless, as a
British historian, writing for an English-speaking audience, I would be per-
verse not to make use of the wonderful source material available regarding the
British Army's use of the machine gun. Furthermore, the Western Front was
the 'engine' of the war; not only in a strategic sense, but also in the field of
tactics. Tactical innovations did of course take place on other fronts, but I
would argue that they are notable largely because they are exceptions to this
rule. Therefore I hope that readers will forgive the consequent weighting of the

contents of this book in favour of the battlefields of France and Belgium. Furthermore, for reasons of space, I have been obliged to limit the compass of the book somewhat, by excluding the activities of some of the smaller combatant armies, along with the whole of the war outside Europe. Finally, I have not attempted to cover the those important outlets for machine gun firepower offered by military aviation and the development of tanks – despite the fact that the latter were originally crewed by the Heavy Branch of the Machine Gun Corps.

I have based this study on what I hope to be a firm grasp of the technology involved; although I freely admit that I would have been ignominiously 'Returned to Unit' from any machine gun training course of the era. A recurring weakness in many publications, including some of great merit, that touch upon the subject of machine guns (or indeed firearms in general) is that the arguments presented are undermined by a basic lack of understanding of the weapons in question. To quote French historians Stéphane Audoin-Rouzeau and Annette Becker:

> It is striking how much historians, though they profess to be discussing the war, are cut off from areas of relevant knowledge. Weapons for example – how they are used, how they work, and what effect they have – are outside the competence of most of them.[13]

I have therefore not flinched from inflicting a substantial amount of technical information upon the reader – although hopefully in a format which is readily understandable. I base this hope on that fact that it is all comprehensible to my none-too-scientific brain.

The title of the book is allusive of the fact that its contents are not limited to the use of machine guns *in* the Great War. Some attention will also be given to the origins of automatic small arms, and the influence that the war had on their subsequent development. Additionally some consideration will be given to the way in which these weapons have been perceived over the course of the 125 years of their existence. Naturally the opinions and recollections of machine-gunners and other soldiers of the First World War are invaluable in providing a human context for the weapon systems. They can also throw a surprising amount of light on technical matters: these men took their trade seriously. However, I have not limited my research to people and events at the Front. The way in which the machine gun was perceived *outside* the military is central to our understanding of its development as such a potent symbol of the Great War. In this respect, certain sections of this book stand at the point where history blurs into the emergent discipline of material culture studies. The machine gun offers a most rewarding subject for study from this perspective.

The study of material culture has its origin in anthropology, but lends itself readily to multidisciplinary use. Fundamentally, it focuses on the way in which humans interact with inanimate objects – imposing on them a constantly changing significance, and charging them with emblematic or even iconic connotations. As should be clear from this book – even, perhaps, from this Prologue alone – the machine gun is a particularly potent example of material culture. I have deliberately avoided corralling this element of the book into an anthropological 'ghetto' at the end. First, the crossover with apparently straightforward matters of history is too indistinct to make this possible. Secondly, I firmly believe that a multidisciplinary approach does greater justice to the subject matter. The machine gun cannot be successfully studied as an item of material culture without a good understanding of its qualities and its combat use. Likewise, if we wish fully to comprehend the legacy of the use of machine guns in the Great War, we must, I believe, be prepared to move beyond the strict confines of history: for that is where their iconic significance has its being.

Chapter 1

A Revolution in Infantry Firepower:
1883–1914

A year ago people in military circles were not so conscious of the
value of machine guns as they are today. Then there were many
people, even in the German Army, who still regarded the machine
gun as a weapon for use against Hereros and Hottentots.

(Matthias Erzberger, 1908)

All sources agree in their ignorance of the precise moment at which the first
true machine gun was discharged. All that can be deduced was that the event
took place during the summer of 1883, at 57d Hatton Garden in the East
Central postal district of London. Here, on the north-western fringes of the
City of London, in an area more usually associated with the jewellery trade,
stood a workshop rented by an American, Hiram Maxim. At some point during
the period in question, which Maxim's own memoirs fail to record with any
precision, he placed six cartridges in an apparatus that discharged them automatically, upon a single trigger pull. In that instant the face of warfare was
changed forever. The inventor himself did not stop to ponder what he had
done, but relates: 'I was delighted. I saw certain success ahead, so I worked day
and night on my drawings until they were finished and went into the shop and
worked myself until I had made the gun.' So familiar have we become with
automatic weapons that it is hard now to conceptualize the veritable quantum
leap in technology that Maxim's invention represented. Even before he had
refined his design, he rendered obsolete in a single sweep all previous 'machine'
gun designs. These weapons, such as the Gatling, the Gardner and the
Nordenfelt, all relied upon manual cranks or levers to operate them. They were
notorious for their tendency to jam at crucial moments – generally due to the
difficulties of feeding ammunition into, and extracting spent cartridges from,
their multiple barrels. These guns were also entirely reliant for their effect on
the strength, stamina and continued survival of the men working their mechanisms – something that could only be done from an exposed, standing position. Their tendency to move in sympathy with the vigorous actuation of their
mechanism also made them inherently inaccurate.

We can presume that the first burst of truly automatic fire was discharged in the basement with which the workshop was furnished and probably during the day. Had the sound of gunfire been noticed and the police called, we would certainly have been told of the event in Maxim's splendidly anecdotal, discursive and, ultimately, evasive memoir *My Life*. The date can be deduced from patent number 3493, which Maxim registered on 16 July 1883 for 'an invention of improvements in machine or battery guns, and in cartridges for the same and other firearms'. The broad terms of this patent were not the product of chance. Maxim was astute enough to realize that, as he later explained to an audience at the Royal United Services Institute: 'No one had ever made an automatic gun before: the coast was clear. Consequently I was able to take out any number of master patents, to show every conceivable way of working an automatic gun and to get very broad claims.' It is indicative of the fertility of Maxim's mind that this raft of patents did indeed cover every way that has ever been employed to operate automatic weapons by the energy generated by the firing of a cartridge.

Hiram Stevens Maxim had arrived in England in August 1881. He was already an established inventor, with over eighty US patents filed in his name. He later admitted to being 'a chronic inventor'. Commencing in his youth with a mousetrap, his inventions ranged from pioneering gas and electrical apparatus, through weapons and explosives, to a steam-powered flying machine. One of his final creations, of which he was uncommonly proud, was a menthol inhaler device for fellow sufferers of bronchial disorders. This was successfully marketed under the somewhat ironic appellation: 'Sir Hiram Maxim's Pipe of Peace'. It was Maxim's success as an inventor in his native USA that led to him becoming domiciled in and, eventually, naturalized and knighted in Great Britain. His persistence in coming up with new electrical devices proved such a thorn in the side of the fledgling American electrical industry that, according to at least one account, the afflicted companies combined to make Maxim an offer that he could not afford to refuse. In return for a 'salary' of $20,000 per annum, he would go to Europe for ten years, ostensibly to report upon European electrical developments. However, a significant clause in the agreement stipulated that he would abstain from any further electrical inventing of his own. His first stop was Paris where, he was later to claim, he met 'An American Jew whom I had known in the states' who told him: 'Hang your chemistry and electricity! If you wish to make a pile of money, invent something that will enable these Europeans to cut each other's throats with greater facility.' This much quoted remark is typical of the kind of anecdote that Maxim loved, but might well be taken with a pinch of salt.

Maxim's own account of his life leaves the reader in no doubt that he was a most remarkable man. A virtually self-taught (actually described as 'semi-literate' by one biographer) genius, he was far from the popular image of an 'inventor'. He was an inveterate practical joker and displayed a somewhat carefree attitude to matrimonial legalities. A physically imposing figure and something of a braggart, his account of his early years contains as many fist-fights as inventions. Even in middle age he was capable of picking up an insubordinate employee and hurling him bodily through a door. Maxim was born in 1840 in the backwoods of Maine, where religious zealots, bears and Native Americans (in descending order of dangerousness) numbered among his childhood neighbours. It was an extraordinary beginning for a man who would later further so many modern technologies. The reader is still more amazed to learn of the practical skills which Maxim employed to bring his inventions to fruition. A fine draughtsman, he could work wood or metal and handle chemicals with equal facility. In short he was a man of a type that simply would not exist today. However, as a source of hard information on weapons technology, *My Life* is a disappointment. Apart from the details of the author's youthful pugilistic triumphs, much of the book is taken up with expatiations about his pet hates – lawyers and the drunken and feckless 'British workman'. Assessment of Maxim's attitude to the death-dealing nature of his creation is also difficult to achieve through analysis of his own words, although he does wryly comment on the fact it was this particular invention which elevated him to 'the pinnacle of fame. Had it been anything else but a killing machine very little would have been said of it.' Maxim was to die in November 1916. His views on the impact of his weapon on the Great War are unrecorded.

The patenting of Maxim's first gun, which he dubbed 'The Forerunner', was just the start of a lengthy process of development that he undertook before 'launching' his 'product'. The 'Forerunner' in fact worked in a completely different fashion from his later guns. He was not satisfied with it and over the ensuing months created a new machine gun – eventually to become known as 'The Prototype'. The first firing of this weapon took place on 24 January 1884. The date is known because the spent cases of the first two cartridges fired are preserved in the Imperial War Museum. The 'Prototype' harnessed the energy of the recoil forces released by firing to cycle its action. Maxim had already patented this means of operating a self-loading weapon, although he appears originally to have envisaged it being used in a rifle. A public announcement of the existence of the new weapon was made, via the press, on 10 October 1884. It made an immediate impact on London society and many powerful and influential men were drawn to Hatton Garden to inspect this marvel. Among those impressed by it were businessmen Albert Vickers (a director of the steel company of the same name) and Randolph Symon, who joined with Maxim to set up the Maxim Gun Company, which was incorporated on 5 November 1884. Maxim then embarked upon a series of journeys to present his invention to the leaders of foreign powers.

A triumph of engineering

By 1887 Maxim had arrived, via a 'Transitional' model, at what he regarded as his 'Perfected' gun. Its system of operation was to become, with minor variations, standard in all Maxim guns and Maxim derivatives. Maxim's stroke of genius, as previously noted, was to power his gun by harnessing the energy released by the firing of a cartridge. In the case of the 'Perfected' gun, this energy was transferred via the recoil movement of the barrel. The action of the weapon is most easily understood if broken down into a sequence of operations, although in fact they all take place within a split second. First a general description of the gun is necessary. The working parts of the gun are either contained in, or mounted upon, what is known as the *receiver*. From the front of the receiver projects the *water-jacket*, which contains water for cooling the barrel and a steam tube for venting it when it boils. The barrel lies in the bottom of the water-jacket, resting in bearings in the front of the water-jacket and the front of the receiver. Above the rear of the barrel sits the *feed block*, which draws belts of ammunition through itself.

It should be understood that any weapon firing powerful ammunition such as military rifle cartridges must have its breech securely closed at the moment of firing. Should this not be the case the spent case will be forced out of the chamber by the expanding gases in the barrel, thus endangering the firer or, at the very least, causing the rupture of the unsupported cartridge case and probably jamming the weapon.

The breech of the Maxim gun is locked by means of a toggle mechanism consisting of two rods linked by a pin (see Plate 2). The rear section of the toggle, known as the *crank*, is anchored to a roller, which is itself linked to the cocking handle or (more properly) *crank handle* on the right of the receiver; the front section engages with the *lock*, which contains the gun's firing mechanism. The toggle is best visualized as a human arm with the lock as its hand and the axis of the crank and crank handle as its shoulder. At the moment of firing the arm is held stiff and straight; forcing the lock against the face of the breech. Upon firing, the barrel and lock recoil together for a short distance. The time taken by this movement is sufficient for the bullet to leave the barrel and the gas pressure therein to drop to a safe level. At this juncture *extension plates* attached to the barrel come into contact with fittings at the rear of the gun, halting the rearward movement of the barrel. Simultaneously, as the crank handle moves backwards, it is cammed upwards by the fixed *roller*: this results in a downward leverage being applied to the crank, which 'breaks' the toggle, which, to continue the human arm simile, it is now bending at the elbow.

With the toggle 'broken' the lock, leaving behind the halted barrel, continues its rearward movement. As the crank turns with the movement of the lock, it tensions a spring – the *fusee* spring – which lies alongside the left of the receiver, thus storing the recoil energy for use in the return part of the action's cycle. As the recoiling parts near the end of their travel, the cleverly engineered relationship between the crank, crank handle and roller transfers the energy of the recoiling lock into forward pressure on the barrel extension plates – thus returning the barrel to its firing position. The fusee spring then pulls the lock back into *battery* (i.e. into its locked position). As this happens a device known as the *check lever* engages with the crank handle to perform the vital function of preventing the lock from slamming against the breech face and 'bouncing' back, which would leave the breech unlocked.

Ammunition is fed into the gun by a fabric belt. This is pulled through the feed block by a mechanism actuated by a protrusion on one of the barrel extensions which projects upwards into the feed block. On the face of the lock is the *extractor*, which is able to slide up and down. This takes the form of a flat plate with in-turned flanges for gripping the bases of cartridges. When the lock is in battery the extractor simultaneously grips the base of the cartridge in the chamber and another one in the belt. At the moment of firing, the firing pin projects through a hole in the face of the extractor. The lock incorporates a mechanism which cocks the firing pin during its rearward movement. At the rearmost point of the lock's travel, the extractor slides down the face of the lock. When the lock returns to battery it simultaneously inserts the new cartridge into the chamber and the spent case into an ejector tube in the lower front of the receiver. At the same instant it is cammed upwards, sliding off the base of the spent case, and over the base of a new round in the belt. This once again aligns the firing pin hole with the firing pin, which (should the trigger remain pressed) springs forward to fire the newly chambered cartridge and the whole process recommences.

Dolf Goldsmith, doyen of machine gun experts, offers an eloquent summation of the Maxim action:

> Maxim was the first to make a single-shot, locked firing mechanism move by the force of its own recoil and contact various other parts, thus enabling it to fire, unlock, extract, eject, cock, feed, chamber and lock again into battery; altogether the most remarkably innovative engineering accomplishment in the history of firearms.[1]

In 1888 Maxim expanded his business base by amalgamating with the rival Nordenfelt Guns and Ammunition Company. The deal was brokered by the greatest arms dealer of the age, Sir Basil Zaharoff, who had spent the preceding four years attempting to sell the lever-operated Nordenfelt gun in competition with the Maxim and had obviously seen the technological 'writing on the wall'. However, by this date, another major change had occurred in the field of firearms technology – one which would greatly enhance the capabilities of the machine gun.

A technological leap

The introduction into service of the French Model 1886 rifle signalled the beginning of a new epoch in the history of warfare. While the rifle itself was unexceptional in its design, the cartridge for which it was chambered was revolutionary. Prior to 1886, rifles and machine guns employed ammunition filled with gunpowder. Typically of calibres ranging from 9.5mm to 12mm, they fired unjacketed lead bullets that followed markedly curved trajectories and were potentially lethal out to around 1,500m. Military experts throughout Europe had long sought to improve on this level of performance. Their goal was to create high-velocity ammunition. Not only would this offer greater range, but the bullets would travel on a much flatter trajectory; thereby greatly simplifying the process of taking accurate aim. Their problem was one of simple physics. To fire a bullet at higher velocity would require either more propellant or a smaller bullet. Increasing the gunpowder charge was not feasible without increasing the recoil of the weapon to unacceptable levels. Conversely, a decrease in calibre was also impossible, as the residues left by gunpowder quickly fouled the barrels of small calibre weapons.

The answer to this conundrum was found during 1884–5 by the French chemist Paul Vieille, who invented a nitrocellulose-based propellant which combusted completely upon firing, releasing a great amount of energy without creating significant residue or smoke. The powder was subsequently christened *Poudre B*, in honour of the flamboyant Minister for War, General Georges Boulanger – a man who was being talked of as a potential new Bonaparte. It was Boulanger who ordered the immediate (not to say precipitate) development of a rifle to chamber a new 8mm cartridge filled with the miraculous propellant. The hasty development meant that the new ammunition was not to be accompanied by a similarly advanced rifle. Furthermore the cartridge itself was fundamentally a 'necked-down' modification of the existing 11mm French service cartridge. Nevertheless, the appearance of the first prototype effectively rendered all other rifles (not to mention machine guns) in service obsolete.[2] The military establishments of the 'civilized world' soon found themselves

embroiled in an infantry weapons 'race' as they vied with each other to intro-
duce small calibre rifles into service. These weapons were of 6.5mm to 8mm in
calibre, and fired bullets that were jacketed with soft metal to prevent their
bores from being fouled with lead. They were typically sighted out to 2,000m,
although their bullets were potentially lethal at even greater ranges.

The invention of smokeless ammunition gave a massive fillip to the development of the machine gun. Maxim had himself been conducting experiments
with smokeless powder, as sustained firing of the black-powder (as gunpowder
now became known) cartridges in his gun, even in the large British .450 calibre,
resulted in serious fouling of the barrel. Furthermore, gunpowder created a
great deal of smoke, which both obscured the vision of those firing and
infallibly gave away their position to the enemy. This was a bad enough problem for rifle-armed infantrymen, but a far more serious one for machine guns,
which of course generated the same amount of smoke as a whole company of
riflemen, but concentrated in one spot. The new cartridges produced less recoil
energy than their predecessors, so Maxim was obliged to rejig the internal
mechanism of his guns accordingly. However, his efforts were well rewarded,
as the performance of the guns benefited hugely from this revolution in ammunition. It was the worldwide adoption of smokeless propellant that paved the
way for the elevation of the machine gun from something of a novelty to an
integral part of virtually every major army.

First blood
The first major order for the 'Perfected' Maxim came from the Austro-
Hungarian Empire, which purchased 131 of them in 1888. In Germany Kaiser
Wilhelm II became personally enthusiastic about the gun after witnessing one
of Maxim's demonstrations of the weapon. He subsequently equipped each of
his Guard Dragoon Regiments with a Maxim at his own expense. However,
official adoption of the Maxim in Germany did not commence until 1894 – by
the Imperial German Navy, rather than by the Army. The other major pur-
chaser of Maxims among the 'Great Powers' was Russia, where they entered
service with the Navy in 1897 and the Army from 1899.

In Britain a somewhat equivocal attitude towards the Maxim developed in
military circles. The superiority of the gun to its manually powered predecessors was acknowledged and, from 1888, numbers of Maxims were
purchased to supplement and, eventually, replace the Nordenfelt and Gardner
guns currently serving with the Army and Navy. By 1904, 1,288 Maxims had
been purchased for the British Army and Royal Navy from Maxim-Nordenfelt
and its successor company Vickers Sons & Maxim. In addition, steps were
taken to arrange the production, under license, of a service Maxim gun at the

Royal Small Arms Factory at Enfield. Production commenced in 1893. However, perhaps due to experience of the unreliability of previous designs, little attempt was made to integrate the Maxim into the infantry tactics of the day. It is suggestive that a high proportion of the first Maxim guns to enter British service did so in the hands of units of Rifle Volunteers (the forerunners of the Territorial Army), who purchased them from their own funds. Other purchases were made by British colonial agencies and it was to be in colonial warfare that the Maxim gun was first fired in anger.

The first actual British use of the Maxim appears to have taken place during a punitive expedition into the Gambia in 1888. The occasion was marked by the personal operation of the Maxim gun in question by a General Officer – Sir Francis de Winton – who successfully took the fortified town of Robari under fire.[3] Another notable early use occurred in 1893, when the Matebele (Ndebele) people of what is now Zimbabwe, clashed with British colonial forces who were seeking to extend their control into Matebeleland. The outnumbered British forces, composed of members of the British South African Police and some volunteers, were equipped with four .450-inch calibre Maxim guns. These brought a devastating fire to bear on the Matabele, who attacked in organized close order formations, hoping to come to close quarters with their assegais. The Matabele nation was crushed and subsumed into the new colony of Rhodesia.[4]

In 1896–9 a still more striking demonstration of the Maxim's worth was given in the Sudan, as Anglo-Egyptian forces, under the British Major-General Horatio Kitchener, attempted to destroy the Mahdiyya – an aggressive Islamic state established in the Sudan by Muhammad Ahmed Al Mahdi, the conqueror of Khartoum. Twenty Maxim guns advanced up the Nile with Kitchener – wrapped in silk to protect their mechanisms from dust and sand. Here, as in Matebeleland, the tactics of the enemy ensured that the Maxims were able to take a dreadful toll of lives. At the climactic battle of Omdurman, in 1898, a German military observer noted the range and effectiveness of a six-gun battery of these .303-inch calibre weapons, when compared with the .450-inch black-powder cartridge rifles of the Egyptian infantry fighting alongside them.

In the same year Hilaire Belloc published his comic poem *The Modern Traveller*, containing the much quoted (usually out of context) lines:

> Thank God that we have got
> The Maxim Gun
> And they have not

The intent was satirical – the whole poem mocks contemporary attitudes, or at least those of the 'Imperialist' press of the day, to colonial affairs. The Maxim also features in the more stridently political writing of anti-imperialist Henry Labouchère, who parodied Rudyard Kipling's call to 'Take up the White Man's burden' with the lines:

> Pile on the Brown Man's burden!
> And if ye rouse his hate
> Meet his old-fashioned reasons
> With Maxims – up to date

This and other examples of Labouchère's poetical invective are reproduced in John Ellis's well-known book *The Social History of the Machine Gun.* In its treatment of the machine gun as an aspect of material culture, this book was a good twenty years ahead of its time, when first published in 1975. However, the handling of much of its subject matter reflects the preoccupations of the preceding decade – particularly with regard to the alleged inability of the 'military mind' to comprehend the usefulness of the new technology. The use of Maxim guns in colonial warfare is discussed in some depth, leading to the conclusion that their importance was played down by those who wished to emphasize traditional martial virtues and the personal, rather than techno-logical, superiority of the white man.

This thesis is not borne out by contemporary reports of these colonial actions, which frequently give prominence to the role of the Maxim gun. It would appear quite clear that the 'up to date' machine gun was accepted as a symbol of Western technological superiority over the less fortunate 'races' of the world. With regard to the suppression of the Matabele, the London *Daily News* was explicit in its view that this was a triumph of technology over courage, asking:

> In how many European armies could the men who had survived one shower from modern artillery come forward to try their luck again? These savages were equal to the attempt, and equal, too, to the deliberate design of bettering their luck by looking for a weak place in the laager. Once more the Maxims swept them down in the dense masses of their concentration, and once more they retired. It seems incredible that they should have mustered for still another attack, yet this actually happened. But this time they reached the limits of human endurance. They came as men foredoomed to failure, and those who were left of them went back a mere rabble rout.[5]

Five years later, the *Daily Telegraph*, reporting on the Battle of Omdurman was moved to assert: 'In most of our wars it has been the dash, the skill, and the bravery of our officers and men that have won the day, but in this case the battle was won by a quiet scientific gentleman living down in Kent.' Maxim would undoubtedly have laughed at his being described as 'quiet', but was by no means lacking in awareness of the benefits that his business might reap from the elevation of his weapon to the status of imperialist icon. In 1888 he earned a great deal of publicity by presenting the explorer Henry Morton Stanley with a special Maxim gun fitted with an 'arrow-proof' shield.

By the end of the nineteenth century, the Maxim had established itself not only as a universally recognizable artefact, but one with generally positive associations; unless, of course, you happened to be one of the indigenous peoples of areas recently incorporated in the British Empire. In 1899 South African impresario Frank Fillis staged an entertainment called 'Savage South Africa' in London. This was a species of African 'Wild West Show' and, in a scene that became the subject of an early film, featured charging Matebele tribesmen (real ones) being dispersed by Maxim fire. A further example of the Maxim's entry into popular culture comes from 1901, when the Vaux brewery of Sunderland launched a new product: Maxim Ale. It was named to celebrate the safe homecoming of Ernest Vaux, a member of the brewing family who had commanded the machine gun section of the Northumberland Hussars in the Boer War. In keeping with the innovative nature of the gun depicted in its advertising, the beer has claims to being the first bottled brown ale ever sold in Britain.

Enthusiasm for the Maxim was not restricted to the British Empire. Maxim himself recorded inspecting postcards in a village shop in Switzerland and finding that:

> on nearly every one of them was a picture of someone firing the Maxim gun. There was a wooden Maxim gun in the little village, and it was considered the thing for visitors to be photographed seated on the gun, with the mountains in the distance.[6]

The Swiss had in fact been among Maxim's earlier customers, purchasing increasing numbers of guns from 1891 onwards.

By 1900 the distinctive silhouette of the Maxim gun had established itself as an image that would remain the predominant generic representation of the machine gun for decades to follow. However, it was no longer the only machine gun available.

The second wave
Even before the first demonstration of the Maxim in Austria-Hungary, two Austrian noblemen, Archduke Karl Salvator and Georg Ritter von Dormus, had come up with a concept for an automatic gun working on the principle of

'delayed blowback'. Blowback is the rearward force exerted on a fired cartridge case as the bullet proceeds up the barrel. This can be utilized to cycle the action of a weapon, but is too dangerous with full powered rifle ammunition (for reasons outlined above). This danger can be averted however, if the opening of the breech can be delayed until pressure in the barrel reaches safe levels. In the Salvator-Dormus design, the delay was achieved by a combination of a powerful spring and the inertia of a pivoting breech block. The weapon was taken up and perfected by the Škoda arms company. Its quirky design and the addition of curious mechanisms for feeding ammunition and regulating its rate of fire made the Škoda gun far less effective than the Maxim. However, as it was an indigenous design, it was adopted by the Austro-Hungarian army, and used in three different variants from 1893 until the First World War.

Another Austrian, Captain Baron Adolf Odkolek von Augezd, was not far behind his compatriots in devising an automatic gun. His design relied upon utilizing the expanding gasses in the barrel to drive a piston to cycle the gun's action. He sold his concept to the Hotchkiss Company of Paris, who perfected the weapon and offered it for sale by the mid-1890s. Unlike the Maxim, the Hotchkiss was an air-cooled weapon and, as such, featured a massive barrel which incorporated 'fins' to increase its external surface area. Instead of fabric belts, it was fed from short metal strips. The air cooling recommended the gun to the French Army, whose colonial commitments often required it to campaign in arid regions. They acquired the Hotchkiss in limited quantities from 1897 onwards. These were employed with some success against the Moors of North Africa. However, use by the 'Metropolitan' French Army was limited to an experimental issue to sixteen battalions of light infantry during 1903–4.

Meanwhile, in the United States, an inventive intellect of a very different stamp was at work. John Moses Browning was born into a family of gunsmiths in Ogden, Utah. His father had been one of the original Mormon pioneers. Unlike his countryman Maxim, Browning's genius lay exclusively in the field of firearms design. But genius it surely was and firearms manufacturers, commencing with Winchester, but later to include Colt and FN of Belgium, were to make fortunes from his designs. Browning became aware of the potential power of the expanding gasses created when a firearm is discharged, and experimented to see if it could be harnessed to work a gun automatically. He first devised a method by which a standard lever-action repeating rifle could be automated. A flapper mechanism was attached to the muzzle of the rifle. The bullet passed through a hole in the flapper, but the expanding gases that followed the bullet drove the flapper forwards to actuate a rod that connected it to the rifle's loading lever. It was not long before Browning applied his concept to a machine gun. In this case the gas was tapped through a hole near the muzzle of the gun to drive down a swinging arm. The arm acted upon a lever, which transferred the gas energy to operate the gun. The design was taken up by the Colt Patent Firearms Manufacturing Company and put into production. It was soon taken into service by the US Navy, as the Colt Model 1895 machine gun. The Colt remained in production until the First World War. Its downward swinging actuating arm could be fouled by the ground if the gun was set up too low, earning it the soubriquet of the 'Potato Digger'.[7]

Both the Colt and the Hotchkiss appeared to have infringed one of Maxim's early patents. Maxim pressed a complaint against Colt with regard to the Browning gun. The US Patent Office however chose to view Browning's design as an adaptation of his own earlier 'flapper' mechanism.[8] Curiously Maxim did not take any action against the Hotchkiss gun when it appeared just two years later, even though it strongly resembled his patented system for gas impinging directly upon a rearward moving piston.

A final addition to the machine guns available in the early years of the twentieth century was the Danish Madsen gun, which qualifies as the first light machine gun ever to enter volume production (although differentiation between machine guns and light machine guns was not made at that time). The Madsen was a unique design, which featured a breech block that pivoted rather than recoiled. It was fired from a light bipod and top-fed from a box magazine. It was named after a Danish War Minister, but designed by Lieutenant Theodor Schouboe. Confusingly it was also known in Britain as the Rexer, after the company that marketed it there. Despite its idiosyncratic system of operation, the Madsen was to remain in production until the 1950s. Incidentally Scandinavia was evidently fertile ground for the propagation of machine guns. As early as 1870, a Swede called Friberg had registered a patent for such a weapon, operated by recoil – being thereby conceptually, if not actually, thirteen years ahead of Maxim. It could not however be made to work until after the invention of smokeless powder. The design was eventually brought to realization in 1907, by Rudolf Henrik Kjellman. Unfortunately the expense of production ensured that only ten Kjellman guns were ever produced.

This 'second wave' of machine gun development heralded a period of change that witnessed a rapid growth in the use and issue of machine guns and of the theoretical basis for their employment. Two early historians of the machine gun, F V Longstaff and A H Atteridge neatly summarized the state of affairs as the nineteenth century drew to a close: 'so far the Maxim Gun had been used almost entirely against the crude tactics of savage or half-civilized opponents. It was still a question what it would do in warfare between regular armies.'

Tactics and procurement

An early opportunity to find the answer came during the opening stages of the Second Boer War of 1899–1902. Unlike their black African neighbours, the Boers did not obligingly attempt to storm British positions. They preferred to rely upon dispersed formations and long-range marksmanship. Against such distant and well-concealed targets British machine gun techniques had, as yet, no answer. Although plenty of Maxims were available, their crews suffered heavily from Boer fire as they tended to be set up as part of the infantry firing line, making them an easy target. A lecturer at the Army School of Musketry was later to assert that 'the numerous complaints received of the gun's action in South Africa were almost certainly due to want of training and supervision of the detachments'.[9] Some Volunteer units equipped themselves with privately purchased Colt or Hotchkiss guns. The Royal North Devon Hussars are known to have acquired a Rexer (Madsen) gun.[10] Another, somewhat surprising, example was offered by the 2nd Baron Kesteven, who personally purchased a Colt gun as an inducement to allow him to serve in South Africa.[11] He subsequently did so as a subaltern, despite being over fifty – coincidentally serving alongside Major Ernest Vaux in the Northumberland Hussars. In the early stages of the war, before their regular forces were driven from the field, the Boers too had a few Maxims and Colts. They also deployed a number of large Maxim 'Pom Poms', which fired an explosive 1lb (37mm) shell. The British Army had rejected proposals to deploy 'Pom Poms' – much to Maxim's disgust – for the sound reason that a field gun was not much bigger and packed a much greater punch. Those 'Pom Poms' that did find their way into British Army service were employed on the Home Front as anti-aircraft guns during the First World War.

Apart from proving the inadvisability of exposing machine guns in the infantry firing line, the Boer War offered few lessons in their use. Thus the officer classes of every Western nation during the opening years of the twentieth century remained united in their ignorance as to what machine gun tactics might be suitable for use against the troops of a 'civilized' power. This situation was soon to change however, due to events in far away Manchuria. The Russo-Japanese War of 1904–5 saw significant use of machine guns by both sides. The Russians were equipped with Maxims built under licence in Germany. Each division was equipped with an eight-gun battery. Their cavalry also deployed a few Madsens. The Japanese used Hotchkiss guns. Initially these were issued only to their cavalry brigades, but as the war progressed each infantry regiment received three or more guns. The machine-gunnery of both sides evolved during the course of the war; there being nothing like actual combat for accelerating the evolution of tactics. The Russians quickly discovered that the high, wheeled carriages of their Maxims made them extremely vulnerable to enemy fire. Soon their soldiers were improvising lower carriages and sleds. This lesson was evidently well learnt, as the Russian-built M1905 Maxim was equipped with a much handier, low (although still wheeled) mount. They were, nevertheless, enthusiastic in their praise of the capabilities of the Maxim. It proved particularly effective in the defence of Port Arthur. One witness recorded the fate of 400 Japanese infantrymen attempting to take cover in a trench during an assault. They were taken in enfilade by two Maxims that had been concealed on a nearby hill.

> Within a few seconds it was turned into a veritable pandemonium, a seething mass of humanity, where men were wildly fighting to get away, trampling on the wounded, climbing over piles of corpses, which blocked the entrance, and trying to escape down the coverless hillside. But the Maxims did their work as only Maxims can, and within a few moments practically the entire force was wiped out.[12]

The Russians concentrated on developing the defensive firepower of the Maxim, preferring short-range fire. The Japanese, due to the strategic impera- tives of the war, were obliged to develop tactics for the offensive use of machine guns. A German observer noted that in an action at Mukden 'all the machine guns of a whole Japanese division were brought into action upon a Russian *point d'appui*. The Russian fire was silenced, but burst out again when ever the machine-gun fire slackened. The Japanese infantry used pauses in the enemy's fire to press forward to close range under cover of their machine-gun fire.'[13] It was also noted that Japanese techniques included fire conducted over the heads of their own attacking troops and night firing, although the intricacies of the Hotchkiss gun's strip-feed system necessitated the introduction of shaded lamps by which to conduct the latter.

A great many foreign observers joined the armies of both sides – one of the most notable being Lieutenant-General Sir Ian Hamilton; later to command the forces landed at Gallipoli. The armies of Europe have been criticized, undoubtedly with some justification, for not applying the lessons of the Russo-Japanese War to their own plans for future European conflicts. Indeed the Russo-Japanese war prefigured the Great War in many ways, with artillery and machine guns dominating the battlefield and much fighting being conducted from entrenched positions. However, it should be noted that open battles took place (temporary entrenchments were no novelty) and the front lines did not congeal in the same way as they did in the autumn of 1914. Furthermore, it is evident that the war in Manchuria represented a watershed in the attitude of European armies towards the machine gun. A French general declared that

'After this war – and especially with soldiers more nervous and less phlegmatic than the Russians – like it or not, one must encumber oneself with this new device if one is likely to face an adversary who possesses it.'[14] A British infantry officer of the period recalled that 'The Russo-Japanese War had ... drawn attention to the great latent possibilities of the automatic, and many soldiers were beginning to study and interest themselves in the matter.'[15] Thus the period from 1906 to 1914 was to see considerably more attention paid to the machine gun than had been witnessed during the preceding twenty years of the weapon's existence. It should be noted however, that official interest in developing suitable tactics for their use lagged considerably behind the pace of the adoption and issue of the weapons themselves. As one American historian has pithily observed: 'The machine gun remained chiefly an asset to be acquired in the expectation that awful consequences might follow if it were not.'[16]

An immediate reaction to the Russo-Japanese War was the acceptance of the principle that the machine gun should become a standard item of issue to the infantry. Prior to the war, only Britain had followed this rule, with other countries issuing them on an experimental basis only. The prime example of this change is offered by the German Army, which had initially been hesitant about the adoption of machine guns. In 1904, one officer recorded his opinion that a single battery of machine guns per Army Corps was a sufficient level of issue. This attitude underwent a radical alteration from 1905 onwards, as reports of the fighting in Manchuria were assimilated. In 1908 Deputy Matthias Erzberger, speaking in the Reichstag alluded to this change, stating that:

> A year ago people in military circles were not so conscious of the value of machine guns as they are today. Then there were many people, even in the German Army, who still regarded the machine gun as a weapon for use against Hereros and Hottentots.

Erzberger and Socialist Deputy, Karl Liebknecht (two men who were destined to play important but murderously curtailed roles in the immediate post-war history of their country), were questioning a Reichstag vote of funds for the procurement of machine guns. They claimed that this was a response to false reports in French newspapers of a French decision to increase their own level of machine gun issue. Apparently the reports originally emanated from the German licensees of the Maxim patent – Deutsche Waffen-und Munitions-fabriken (DWM). Some have seen in this subterfuge the hand of none other than the 'Merchant of Death' Sir Basil Zaharoff, who had an interest in DWM.[17] It is clear however, from other German sources of the period, that a general fear of losing a machine gun 'arms race' with France was a major motivation for German spending in this period. In 1907 there were insufficient funds to underwrite the Army's desire to issue six guns per infantry regiment. A target of a mere six per brigade was set instead – with the programme not commencing until 1911. The heightened international tension following the Moroccan Crisis of 1911 changed all this. A new Army Bill of 1912 finally recognized the Army's need for six guns per regiment.[18]

The year 1908 had seen the introduction of a new lightened Maxim gun for the German Army, the MG08. This would remain the standard German machine gun until the 1930s. It was accompanied by a sophisticated quadripod mount, often referred to as the *schlitten*, due to its ability to be dragged like a sledge if its front legs were folded back. The same year saw the issue of a new set of field service regulations, which covered machine gun use in some detail. Generous scales of ammunition issue promoted good training. Additionally, 1,000 rounds were allotted to each new gun, simply to enable their idio-syncrasies to become known to their users, for, just like artillery pieces, machine guns display individual characteristics in the way that they shoot. Importantly, machine-gunners were treated as specialists and, once trained, remained machine-gunners for the rest of their military career, even after passing into the Reserve. These developments did not pass unnoticed abroad. The British General Staff *Handbook of the German Army* of 1914 stated that: 'Germany is evincing her belief in the value of machine-guns by the great increase she has made, from 1905 to 1913, in the numbers of these weapons allotted to her field armies, and in the attention paid to the training of the personnel'. By August 1914, the Germany field army appears to have deployed around 2,500 machine guns, with up to 1,000 others dispersed in fortified localities.[19]

It would be an understatement to say that the army of the Austro-Hungarian Empire does not feature heavily in Anglophone historiography. Consequently it is almost a surprise to discover that the Habsburg Empire was an early leader in the field of machine-gunnery. In 1906 the Kaiserlich und Königlich army established a machine gun school at Bruck-an-der-Leitha. Although Austria-Hungary possessed a significant modern industrial capacity, the equipment of the army was not a priority for the treasury. This led to delays in the devel-opment of new artillery and re-equipment with the new Model 1895 rifle. This neglect was to have serious consequences for the effectiveness of the army in 1914. However, the situation with regard to machine guns appears to have been rather better. There was evidently a swift realization that the curious Škoda machine gun was not capable of development into a truly effective weapon. Therefore, in 1907, a far superior design was adopted: the Schwarzlose.

Designed by German-born Andreas Schwarzlose, this weapon was manufactured by Austria's main arms maker, Waffenfabrik Steyr. Most unusually for a machine gun, it works on the blowback principle, with the breech never being locked. In order to ensure safe functioning, the breech block and mainspring are heavy. Additionally a toggle arrangement helps to retard the blowback by obliging the recoiling parts to overcome a mechanical disadvantage. The advantage of the system is its simplicity, ruggedness and the fact that its mechanism requires only one spring. Unfortunately it was also found necessary to lubricate the cartridges used, as the violent and sudden extraction of the spent case, which was inherent in the system, would otherwise rupture the cases. This was initially achieved by an integral oiler, although this was replaced in Schwarzlose guns made after 1912 with an oiled pad. Another disadvantage was the fact that the barrel of the weapon needed to be relatively short to prevent dangerously high gas pressure building up within it. This circumscribed the accuracy of the gun at long range.

The Schwarzlose was, nevertheless, an efficient weapon and remained in service with various armies until after the Second World War. Nor were the Austro-Hungarian military backward in issuing the weapon to their troops. By 1914 each infantry regiment was (at least theoretically) furnished with four two-gun machine gun sections – one section per battalion. A liberal allowance of ammunition was made for training purposes. The machine gun school at Bruck published bi-monthly reports on machine gun handling; some of them based on fire observation experiments carried out in snowfields. On the outbreak of war the Austro-Hungarian Army had 2,761 machine guns on issue.

In the French Army matters were, contrary to German fears, progressing at a much slower pace. Although a proven design, the Hotchkiss, was available, it was not adopted for general issue. A French machine gun historian has recently neatly summarized that situation:

> Unfortunately, Hotchkiss was a private company, the inventor of its gun was a foreigner, and its development had been conducted by a team composed of French and American civilians! This was too much for the French Army, with whom the culture of secrecy was already taken to the extreme.[20]

Consequently the French Army decided that it must develop its own machine gun. They stipulated that the gun should be air-cooled and that the rate of fire should be easily alterable. These requirements were best met by a gas-operated gun with a changeable barrel. By 1905 the state arsenal at Puteaux had created a gun which it was hoped would fit the bill. This was an extraordinary weapon, which employed the muzzle blast to blow-*forward* a nose-cap, which was attached to a rod. The rod was used to cycle the action of the gun, with its forward movement being transformed into rearward pressure on the breech block by a pivoting yoke device. The gun boasted the dubious advantage of having a cyclic rate of fire adjustable between 8 and 650 rounds per minute. It was soon realized that the Puteaux gun was markedly inferior to the commercial Hotchkiss. It suffered greatly from overheating – a problem not alleviated by the presence of a finned bronze 'radiator' around the barrel, which tended to crack at high temperatures. The overheating caused severe barrel wear and, to cap it all, it was discovered that the solid brass French *Balle D* bullet made the barrel unusable after 3,000 rounds had been fired.

The Puteaux gun was produced in small numbers between 1905 and 1907 – around 300 remained in service in 1914. However, the tardiness of the French Government in arranging adequate provision of machine guns for its troops had, by this time, come to the notice of the Chamber of Deputies – largely due to the efforts of Deputy Charles Humbert. He published, to great public interest (and, let it be said, to the probable benefit of his own financial interests in the 'defence industry'), a pamphlet entitled *Sommes-nous défendus?* The resulting furore threatened the Government with a vote of no confidence, forcing it, among other things, to promise to push forward with the manufacture and distribution of machine guns.

From 1907 onwards the French Army proceeded to adopt a 'product-improved' version of the Puteaux, which had evolved at another government arsenal: that of St Etienne. The M1907 St Etienne gun was more conventional than the Puteaux gun, as it tapped gas from a port midway along the barrel. However, the needless complications of the blow-forward mechanism and the adjustable rate of fire were retained. In the St Etienne the forward movement of the operating rod was reversed by a rack and pinion mechanism that acted upon the breech block. The overheating problem was not entirely resolved and the proximity of the mainspring to the barrel exacerbated this fault, as the spring tended to lose its temper when heated. Nonetheless, the St Etienne remained the standard French service machine gun at the outbreak of war in 1914. From 1910 onwards it was issued on a scale of two guns per battalion. It is indicative of the French Army attitude to machine guns that scale of ammunition issue for machine gun training stood at about half the level enjoyed by German machine-gunners. Nevertheless, it is interesting to note the French Army of August 1914 was in possession of greater numbers of machine guns than its enemy. In fact it had at its disposal over 5,000 guns, although 2,880 of these were deployed in fortresses rather than with the army in the field (many of the fortress guns would have been of the old Puteaux type).[21]

The Russian Army remained wedded to the Maxim gun. They had been impressed with the performance of the weapon in their war with Japan and, from 1907, commenced manufacture of their own licence-built model at the Tula Arsenal. At the same time, the cumbersome wheeled carriages which had caused problems during the 1904–5 war were replaced by a new type of mount. The low, wheeled mount designed by Colonel A A Sokolov has since become synonymous with the Russian use of the Maxim. It could be dragged by one or two men and featured folding legs, which enabled it to be swiftly converted into a tripod. Production of the M1905 Maxim and its lightened successor the M1910 was carried out at an impressive pace and, by the outbreak of war, Russia could field around 5,000 of these weapons. This figure compares most favourably with the numbers available to other armies, but needs to be set in the context of the huge army of over three million men which Russia expected to mobilize in the event of war.

The English-speaking nations were more tentative in their adoption of machine guns. Ironically, in light of the nationality of both Maxim and Browning, the USA must certainly be considered as the back-marker in the race to exploit the potential of automatic firepower. The US Army had in fact adopted the Maxim for service in November 1904, but by 1908 had acquired only 287 of them. Of these guns, ninety were purchased from Vickers Sons and Maxim, while Colt manufactured the rest under licence. The Maxim was not universally popular within the US Army. The cavalry in particular found it, with its attendant mount and requirement for water, too cumbersome. In 1909 the Maxim was superseded by the Benét-Mercié Machine Rifle. This weapon was nothing other than a lightened variant of the Hotchkiss machine gun, fired from a light bipod. It took its name from Hotchkiss employees Henri Mercié and Laurence V Benét. The latter was an American and the son of a former head of the US Ordnance Department.

Whether the family background of Benét was an aid to the adoption of his gun is open to question. However it would seem clear that the main reason that its procurement was permitted to proceed was the fundamental lack of a doctrine for machine gun use within the US Army. The bipod mounted Benét-Mercié could never fulfil the role of a true machine gun like the Maxim but it was liked for its portability. In any case the US Cavalry did not envisage the use of such weapons at ranges in excess of 1,000 yards.

Notwithstanding this sorry state of affairs, the US Army did in fact produce an early 'prophet' of machine-gunnery, in the form of Captain John H Parker. Parker had commanded a detachment of Gatling guns in Cuba, during the Spanish-American War of 1898. The fact that such hand-cranked weapons were still in front-line service at this late date speaks volumes about the attitude of his superiors to the Maxim gun. Parker, however, grasped the potential of the new technology and published papers encouraging its increased use. Among other things, he advocated the creation of a separate corps to use the machine gun and warned of the danger that 'attention may be diverted from the question of organization by the side issue of possible future change of equipment'. Despite his friendship with President Theodore Roosevelt, Parker's pleas made no impact on the army command. The latter, after all, had no realistic expectation of ever being involved in a war with any of the European 'Powers'.[22]

The British Army had of course been an early user of the Maxim. By 1914 over 2,000 had been purchased from commercial sources or manufactured at Enfield. This respectable figure should not be permitted to disguise the fact that a good deal of inertia existed with regard to the development of the machine gun as an integral element of infantry firepower. Some have blamed the Government for failing to respond to military calls for an increased level of machine gun issue, while others contend that the Army did not press such demands with any conviction. Such evidence as exists suggests that the Army was happy, from a tactical viewpoint, with the current scale of issue, but saw the wisdom of building up a reserve of machine guns. The Treasury – led, ironically, by none other than David Lloyd George, who was later to castigate the Generals for being blind to the need for machine guns – declined to fund the creation of such a reserve. There matters were permitted to rest. The Army had little expectation of any long-term involvement in a major European war, while the Treasury was content to channel funds into the building of Dreadnoughts – a relatively cheap alternative to a lavishly equipped army.

Many writers have suggested that the British Army exhibited a particularly hidebound attitude toward the machine gun. They are not limited to those who seek to question the competence of British generalship, but include machine gun 'enthusiasts' aiming to contrast pre-war inactivity with later war-time achievements. Certainly there is a wealth of evidence to suggest that an unfortunately reactionary outlook existed among representatives of all ranks. The British Army was traditionally pervaded by a strong strain of anti-intellectualism and there were many who were averse to cramming their heads with the technical knowledge required for the proper employment of Maxim guns. They were content to put their own construction upon the official description of the machine gun as a 'weapon of opportunity', thinking in terms of using single guns against unruly 'savages'. There were others whose failure to differentiate between modern machine guns and the hand-cranked weapons of old led them to place 'an over-insistence upon the delicacy of the mechanism'. Finally there were those who simply refused to countenance the realities of automatic firepower. Sir Edward Spears recalled a severe damp-ening of his youthful enthusiasm as a cavalry machine gun officer. Upon suggesting to his Brigade commander, 'Black Jack' Kavanagh, that he had notionally mowed down the entire Brigade with his guns during manoeuvres, he received the following rejoinder: 'Here is a young cavalry officer who has the impertinence to say that the infantry weapons he is so inappropriately carting about ... has wiped out the 1st Cavalry Brigade, the finest mounted force in Europe. Get off your horse Sir ... and hand it over and walk back to barracks, the proper form of locomotion for you!'

Such anecdotes, amusing though they are, do not paint a complete picture. The Army as a whole was not blind to the potential of machine guns. A number of officers gave lectures and published papers urging both the more general adoption of machine guns and the development of tactics for their use. Prominent among these was a cavalryman, Captain R V K Applin, who called for the training of specialist machine gun officers and theorized about the potentialities of the machine gun in the attack. More influentially (as he was Chief Instructor at the School of Musketry at Hythe) Major N R McMahon was a strong advocate of automatic firepower. Lecturing at Aldershot in 1907, he asserted that:

> There need be no fear of overstating the value of these weapons. All tendencies in modern tactics, night firing, envelopment, avoidance of open ground, cramped fire frontage, cavalry fire action, invisibility and mobile reserves, bring their good qualities more and more into relief.

McMahon and his colleagues had conducted experiments which convinced them that *volume* of fire, rather than accuracy, was the key to achieving 'superiority of fire' on the battlefield – he likened this to historical supremacy of the English longbow over the more accurate, but slower shooting, crossbow. McMahon was thwarted in his wish for more machine guns, but compensated by developing British Army musketry to an extraordinarily high standard, with soldiers expected to be able to deliver fifteen aimed shots in a minute. Mean-while, his work on machine-gunnery was closely studied by the German Army, which had received copies of it as the result of a mutual exchange of military information with Britain. The Germans were eager to ingest such material, as their own machine gun training had in fact got off to a faltering start. In 1910 one officer admitted to a British observer: 'our officers do not yet understand machine guns: they either use them as artillery or infantry'. The observer, Captain Yate, had attended the manoeuvres of the Prussian Guard and stated that 'Nothing that was seen at these manoeuvres created a less favourable impression than the handling of these [machine] guns.' He noticed precisely the same errors of deployment that had been committed in the Boer War – with guns being set up as part of the firing line, with little or no concealment.[23] However the German Army, as an institution, was committed to improving this state of affairs. By contrast, in Britain, the tactical thinking of home-grown machine gun theorists did not find its way into official print, although it was of course available for any interested officer to read.

Slowly, the theoretical seeds sown by these enterprising individuals began to bear fruit. Machine gun training courses were instituted at Hythe. The Indian Army also ran courses at its school at Pachmari. In 1910 an experiment was made in grouping all the machine guns of a brigade together in a single battery. A contemporary machine gun officer expressed his belief that the resulting report 'greatly influenced the future organization, drill, training and equipment of machine gun sections in the infantry, since from this date conditions began steadily to improve and continued to do so up to the outbreak of the Great War in 1914'.[24] Major McMahon was himself an enthusiast for the 'brigading' of machine guns, claiming that they should have 'an organization favourable to massed action when necessary'. As will be seen in the next chapter, failure to heed these words was possibly the greatest failing of the pre-war British Army. The actual scale of machine gun issue closely matched that of other armies of the day, with a two-gun section forming part of each battalion. However, machine guns were still firmly embedded in the infantry battalions (or cavalry regiments) and did not benefit from being commanded by specialist machine gun officers. Such was the position when the British Expeditionary Force embarked for the continent in that fateful August of 1914.

Chapter 2

The Search for Superiority of Fire: 1914–1915

Le feu n'est que l'auxiliaire du mouvement.
(French field service regulations, 1912)

The armies which marched to war in August 1914 were united in their belief that the war would be one in which manoeuvre would bring about a relatively swift decision. While tactical doctrines varied, all were agreed that the final decision in battle would be obtained at bayonet point. Therefore, the proper employment of firepower was to facilitate the decisive assault by destroying or neutralizing the enemy's capacity to resist. In the minds of the generals of 1914, this firepower was to be derived from two sources, artillery and the infantry firing line. Machine guns were seldom considered as anything more than an augmentation of the latter. Despite the Japanese experimentation in Manchuria, the concept of the machine gun as an offensive weapon remained underdeveloped. So, being regarded as essentially defensive weapons, their potential was underestimated by armies wedded to achieving decisions by offensive means.

Artillery was the senior partner in the provision of firepower. Fundamentally this meant field guns of relatively small calibre – from 75mm to 84mm (the latter being the metric calibre of the British 18-pounder). Their size was predicated on the assumption that they would need to keep pace with the infantry while being towed by a small team of horses. Larger guns required more specialized transport arrangements. At shorter ranges, firepower was to be provided by the infantry, who were predominantly armed with the generation of bolt-action rifles that had evolved since the introduction of smokeless powder. These were typically sighted out to 1,500m and, in skilled hands such as those of British Regulars, could discharge as many as twenty aimed shots in a minute. However, it was well known in military circles that the theoretical deadliness of rifle fire was seldom matched by its actual performance in battle. It was estimated that 20,000 rounds of small arms ammunition were expended for each man killed during the Russo-Japanese War. In his book *Firing Line*,

Richard Holmes produced some interesting statistics regarding this phenomenon, including a calculation that, in 1914, a British Guards battalion (boasting
the most accurate musketry in the world) typically expended 24,000 rounds to
cause less than 1,000 casualties. The French field regulations of 1912 warn that
the advance of the infantry constitutes the 'true menace which determines the
retreat of the enemy, *especially as their fire is sometimes not very murderous* [italics
added]'. The reason for this mediocre performance was of course battlefield
stress. Men under fire tended either to become 'drunk on rifle fire', and shoot
incontinently without aiming, or to fire high, or not at all. During the Russo-
Japanese War, it was discovered that the effectiveness of rifle fire actually
showed a sharp decline at ranges of less than 150m, with men becoming
increasingly seized by panic as the enemy closed.

In this context the advantages of the machine gun are obvious. The machine
gun was, in the memorable phrase of Major McMahon, a 'nerveless weapon'.
Once the gun was 'laid' on a target or target area, its firepower could be
developed much more reliably than that of an equivalent number of riflemen
(this number has, incidentally, been variously estimated at anything between
20 and 120 – which shows how notional the concept is). The effects of fear and
confusion on its firers could not readily disturb the aim of a machine gun. As
a British Army training pamphlet was later to put it: 'The accuracy of fire
is increased by a reduction of the personal factor.' With proper preparations
machine guns could even be fired accurately at night. Firing a military rifle of
the period was also a physically demanding activity. While attempting to lodge
himself in whatever cover was available, the firer would have to ignore the
detonations of incoming artillery shells and the ear-splitting reports of the rifles
of his comrades, and squint through sights which were not easy to use even in
perfect conditions. If firing at anything but very short range, he would first
have had to adjust his rear sight accordingly – hopefully correctly. In the act
of pulling the trigger he needed to be sure not to flinch in expectation of more
ear-splitting noise and a sharp thump when the weapon recoiled against his
shoulder. The machine gun offered few of these disadvantages. Once it had
been laid on target, the mount ensured that it maintained its aim. Meanwhile
there was little or no recoil to trouble the gunner.

Machine guns and modernism

The automated nature of this death-dealing combination of man and machine
was not lost on artists of the period. The Futurist movement, which had
formed the avant-garde of the art world in the years immediately preceding the
war, was deeply interested in the notion of mechanization. In his *Futurist
Manifesto* the Italian modernist Filippo Marinetti asserted that 'a roaring motor

car which seems to run on machine-gun fire, is more beautiful than the Victory of Samothrace'. This obsession was to influence artistic depictions of the war. The artists Henri Gaudier-Brzeska and Christopher Nevinson created images of machine-gunners (the former's *La Mitrailleuse en action* and the latter's *La Mitrailleuse*) which conflated the gun with the man. A critic viewing Nevinson's image of French machine-gunners (serving what appears to be a captured German Maxim gun) wrote: 'Are they men? No! They have become machines. They are as rigid and as implacable as their terrible gun. The machine has retaliated by making man in its own image.'[1] This small work, painted during the artist's honeymoon in Ramsgate, made a sensational impact. According to Paul Gough:

> Critical and popular acclaim was unanimous: 'the best and the most ruthless illustration of the menace of this deadly machine war ... produced to date' wrote Charles Lewis Hind as he saluted the 'self-sacrificing automota' captured by Nevinson. Crowds thronged to see it. Gallery attendants were posted to protect it. No lesser a figure than Sickert described it as the 'most authoritative and concentrated utterance on the war in the history of painting'.[2]

Others were drawn to the mechanical aesthetic of the machine gun and its workings. These included Vorticist artists, such as Wyndham Lewis, and more conservative illustrators such as Arthur Bradbury, who were attracted to its hard edges and rigid surfaces as the most relevant subject matter for the mechanical age. Those of a more conventional bent also appear to have been influenced by the Futurist mindset. Edward Handley-Read was an artist who employed his talents during the war to produce technical drawings for the Machine Gun Corps, in which he served as a Sergeant Instructor. He was also responsible for the cover-art of the *Machine Gun Corps Magazine*, but evidently found time to pursue his own artistic career too. He gave his picture of British machine-gunners firing their gun the forbidding title: 'Killing Germans: The Machine at Work'. This impression of the machine gun was not limited to the artistically inclined. Longstaff and Atteridge wax lyrical to the effect that 'its gust of destructive fire has a particularly nerve-shaking quality. Those who have to face it and witness its devastating effect on their comrades have the uncanny feeling that they are up against a machine, not merely fighting with other men.' Marinetti also identified the man-against-machine nature of contemporary combat when he wrote of the Italian war-cry 'Savoia!': 'that rips itself apart and dies heroically in shreds against the mechanical, geometrical, inexorable rolling-mill of the machine-gun fire'.[3]

Issue, organization and doctrine

As indicated in the preceding chapter, the level of machine gun issue in the armies of the major powers in 1914 was roughly equivalent. The Russians were actually the most lavishly equipped on paper, with an eight-gun company attached to each regiment. However this remained a sadly theoretical scale of issue for some Russian regiments, for whom even rifles were a scarce commodity. The Russian Army was 833 machine guns short of its official scale of issue at the outbreak of war. Once the fighting began this situation worsened, as pre-war forecasts of wastage proved to have been far too low. Efforts were made to increase production and to negotiate purchases from abroad. It was not until 1916, however, that production exceeded the average rate of wastage, which stood at 600 guns per month. Russian machine-gunnery was further hampered by a severe shortage of small arms ammunition, which prevailed throughout 1915.[4]

Austria-Hungary, Russia's chief enemy in 1914, also suffered from a shortage of rifles, due to pre-war parsimony. Conversely, small arms ammunition was very plentiful – undoubtedly to the benefit of the machine-gunnery of the Habsburg Empire's armed forces. When their former ally, Italy, attacked in May 1915, machine guns were to prove the mainstay of the successful defensive campaign mounted by the outnumbered Austro-Hungarian forces. They took a particularly high toll of Italian troops attempting to force the valley of the River Isonzo.[5] Italy had rather neglected the machine gun, with only two guns attached to each regiment (which were composed of either three or four battalions). The elite Alpini fared rather better, with two guns per battalion. Italy purchased 892 Vickers 'C' Class machine guns between 1910 and 1914. Reports reaching Britain suggested that they were intended for the defence of Italy's northern frontiers. The coming of war cut off any further possibility of commercial purchases from Britain: such was the need for machine guns in the British Army that selling them to neutral nations was out of the question. Consequently the Italians were obliged to turn to an indigenous design: the Revelli, named for its designer Abiel Bethel Revelli. Like the Schwarzlose, the Revelli worked on the delayed blowback principle, although, just to complicate matters, the barrel also recoiled for a short distance after firing. The delay was effected by a swinging wedge mechanism. In another echo of the Schwarzlose, the cartridges had to be lubricated to ensure clean extraction. The Revelli did not possess the ruggedness of its Austrian counterpart and its potential for unreliability was only enhanced by its use of a unique open magazine, containing fifty rounds. The troubles of Italian machine gunners were compounded by the fact that the Italian Army used a rather underpowered 6.5mm cartridge. As the war progressed the Revelli was supplemented by considerable numbers of the St Etienne gun, supplied by France – thereby augmenting the quantity, if not the quality, of Italian machine guns.

The most effective user of machine guns in the first year of the war was the German Army. German machine-gunners held a decided advantage over their opponents: not because they possessed more guns, but for organizational reasons. Ostensibly the German provision of two guns per battalion matched arrangements in the British and French Armies. However the German guns were organized in a separate company, which was considered the thirteenth company of each three-battalion regiment. This meant that instead of being distributed piecemeal to the three battalions of the regiment, the machine guns remained under the direct control of the regimental commander, and were often grouped together in action. Indeed German regulations specifically stipulated that machine guns should always be under the command of the senior officer present. In addition to the machine gun companies of infantry and cavalry regiments, eleven independent machine gun 'detachments' (*Abteilungen*) were available to corps commanders – these had originally been intended for use in conjunction with the cavalry.

One of the earliest lessons learnt by machine-gunners during the First World War was that this type of 'brigading' of guns could greatly enhance their effectiveness, by concentrating their firepower at crucial points. A clear example of this occurred on 26 August 1914, during the Battle of Tannenberg, when, near that village, a Russian counter-attack was shattered by the concentrated fire of the six machine guns of the German 150th Infantry Regiment.[6] In the West, the battle of Le Cateau witnessed the offensive use of 'closely massed' German machine guns.[7] The Germans went further than other nation in laying down field regulations for the employment of machine guns. Concentration of fire was encouraged and it was considered a 'mistake' to advance machine guns closer to the enemy than 800m if effective supporting fire could be delivered without so doing. Nevertheless, in common with other armies, the Germans still thought in terms of a war of manoeuvre; thus their regulations contained instructions for such activities as firing upon enemy bivouacs by night.

Another advantage held by the Germans was the specialist nature of their machine-gunners and machine gun officers. American historian Dennis Showalter has pointed out that this effect was enhanced in wartime because the limited numbers of trained machine-gunners meant that there was little interchange of machine gun officers and NCOs between first line and reserve regiments (the reverse being the case with their counterparts in rifle companies), therefore 'an active machine-gun company was likely to take most of its peacetime cadre into the field, with corresponding benefits to morale and stability'.

However, before attributing too high a level of preparedness to the Imperial German Army, it would be wise to reflect on what this meant for machine-gunnery in reserve formations, which were expected to fight at the Front and which, in many instances, lacked machine gun companies altogether.[8] This fact, added to the natural wastage of the stock of machine guns that occurred in combat, meant that German divisions in the field were running short of them by the autumn of 1914. Of the eight German divisions primarily involved in the Battle of the Marne (those of III and IX Armeekorps of von Kluck's First Army and X and X Reserve Armeekorps of von Bülow's Second Army), only one could deploy its full complement of machine guns (twenty-four). Others fared less well, with one division having only six – the average per division being fifteen.[9] Shelford Bidwell and Dominick Graham, in their indispensable work *Fire Power*, assert that each German *battalion* was furnished with a machine gun company. This is certainly not so, except in the case of Jäger Battalions, which were not grouped in regiments. This fact is not only implicit in the levels of equipment quoted above, but is also proved by the reliable figure we possess for the total number of guns available (quoted in the previous chapter), which simply would not support such a scale of issue. Contemporary Allied observers certainly did credit the Germans with more Maxim guns than they possessed, with estimates of up to 50,000 being bandied about. This might be taken as a sign of the effective use made by the Germans of the guns that they did have, but was also a consequence of the general pre-war tendency to underestimate the potential effect of machine gun firepower.

The situation in the French Army could hardly have been more different. Although the French level of machine gun issue met the two guns per battalion 'norm' of the period, their policy was to use only one at a time. This was due to the unreliability of their guns. It was thought better to keep at least one gun firing continuously, rather than risk two failing simultaneously.[10] Naturally, the grouping of guns was not a consideration in this context. The reliability problem was not just a fault of the bizarre mechanism of the St Etienne gun. It was a general failing of air-cooled machine guns. Due to the state of metallurgy at that date, air-cooled guns inevitably began to lose accuracy in sustained fire, due to expansion of the barrel. Tests conducted with Hotchkiss guns revealed that the expansion was such that bullets began to fail to take the rifling after three to four minutes of sustained fire. The Colt 'Potato Digger' became dangerously hot after 500 rounds had been discharged. Water-cooling, although more cumbersome, was far more efficient.

Such considerations were of marginal interest to most in the French Army of 1914. Their tactical doctrine was one of attack. The infantry assault with the bayonet was to be pressed home as soon as the enemy's defensive fire had been neutralized. The rifles and machine guns of the infantry would play a part in this neutralization phase, but the main work would be done by the artillery – specifically by the 75mm field gun. The French *Soixante-Quinze* was an excellent weapon, but the reliance that the French placed upon it certainly retarded the development of machine-gunnery in their army. As it turned out, the 75 was found to be vulnerable when brought forward to aid the assault. The Germans had not invested all their hopes in a single weapon system and, although their 77mm field gun could not match the 75, they could engage it in counter-battery fire with the 105mm howitzers with which their infantry divisions were also equipped. Moreover, field guns firing in the open made a tempting target for enemy machine guns.

The situation altered as France was forced onto the defensive. In other armies in 1914 the machine gun came to the fore as the primary source of defensive firepower – indeed the French infantry suffered grievously at the hands of German machine-gunners during the Battle of the Frontiers. However, in the French Army this role was performed with great success by the *Soixante-Quinze*, which could indeed develop a frightening level of destructive power. A four-gun battery of 75s, firing at a rate of ten rounds per minute (just half of the twenty rounds theoretically possible) could put 10,000 shrapnel balls per minute into an area 100m by 400m. That is to say *ten times* more projectiles than four machine guns firing at the standard French *cadence moyenne* of 200–300 rounds per minute. Little wonder that the German soldiers referred to the French gunners, in their dark blue uniforms, as the 'Black Butchers'.

Thus, for the time being, the machine gun remained a mere adjunct of infantry firepower, although the French field regulations made the following succinct differentiation: 'The infantry must advance and shoots to advance; the machine gun must shoot and advances to shoot.' This phrase, agreeably elliptical though it is, cannot mask the fundamental absence of machine gun doctrine in the French Army of 1914.

The BEF: trials and errors
Lieutenant-Colonel Graham Seton Hutchinson, a British machine gun officer who became a historian of machine guns after the war (and who, in a curious parallel with his fellow maverick, Fuller, was to dabble in Fascist politics), summed up the British situation at the outbreak of war as follows: 'The hour of war struck. While the Expeditionary Force mobilized and Lord Kitchener issued his dramatic appeal for a manhood to fight for Britain in the battles of the nations, machine guns were forgotten.' As a leading proponent of machine-gunnery, Hutchinson was probably pitching it a bit strong. However machine guns were certainly viewed by most as merely an adjunct to the British

infantry's impressive rifle firepower and, worse, such machine gun experts as the Army possessed were dispersed when it was decided to close the School of Musketry upon mobilization. The first year of the war was to become a bitter learning experience for British machine-gunners. One officer, writing after the war, stated that:

> machine guns were, in the majority of cases wrongly employed at the outbreak of the war. They were continually pushed forward, often into impossible places, generally against the advice of the expert (the machine gun section commander) where they were at once spotted and just as quickly blown out of existence by opposing artillery. The eight guns of the brigade in which I was serving at this time were reduced to two in a remarkably short period. I attribute this entirely to the above-mentioned method of employment.[11]

He goes on to say that the machine guns were actively hampered in their duty to support the most forward infantry, by being deployed in the midst of those very troops. The officers commanding the machine gun sections were too junior to influence the placement of their guns. The first Victoria crosses to be won in the war were in fact awarded to two machine-gunners as a result of just this sort of misuse. Lieutenant Dease and Private Godley of the Royal Fusiliers won the medal (the former posthumously) for their attempts to man a Maxim gun sited in a horribly exposed position at Mons. Even as late as the Second Battle of Ypres, in the spring of the following year, the 'suck it and see' approach to machine gun deployment was evident. Bruce Bairnsfather, the creator of 'Old Bill', fought at that battle as a machine gun officer with the Royal Warwickshire Regiment. He recalled that:

> We fixed up a couple of machine guns, and awaited a favourable opportunity. I could see lots of Germans running along the front of the wood towards one end of it. We laid our aim on the wood, which seemed to be the chief spot to go for.[12]

Some very basic rules were being ignored. Prominent among these was the fact that the firepower of machine guns is hugely more effective in enfilade (i.e. when fired from a flanking position) than when it is aimed directly into the enemy's front line. It has been recorded (and oft-repeated) that a pre-war machine gun officer, upon requesting orders for his guns, was told to 'take the damned things to the flank and hide 'em' by his superior. In fact, given the tactical precepts of the time, there was no better position for these weapons than concealed on the flank of their parent formation.

This story originated in the book *From Chauffeur to Brigadier* by the splendidly named Brigadier-General Christopher D'Arcy Bloomfield Saltern Baker-
Carr. Formerly on the staff of the School of Musketry, Baker-Carr had retired
from the Army in 1906, but wangled himself a job as a civilian chauffeur in
Flanders in 1914. By a combination of circumstances (and his own determination to play an active role in the war) he was tasked with creating the British
Army's first Machine Gun School. He is therefore an important figure in the
development of machine-gunnery in the British Army. Unfortunately his book
is not entirely trustworthy as an account of events. Not only does the author
display a rather relaxed attitude to the recording of dates, but he also appears
unaware of developments that occurred in his field of expertise during his
eight-year sabbatical from the Army. Furthermore, the whole book is presented as a heroic struggle waged by the author against the dead weight of the
'military mind'. Enriching this heady brew is Baker-Carr's evidently fester-
ing resentment of those who had, unlike himself, attended Staff College. This
makes for lively reading, but unreliable history. However, he makes a significant point about the poor deployment of British machine guns, which
evidently persisted throughout the first year of trench warfare: 'Not one but
dozens of machine gun emplacements did I see in the line which faced directly
to their front, thereby reducing the value of the weapon by anything up to
ninety per cent.'

Ballistics
Before proceeding further, it would be wise to establish just what the 'value' of
a machine gun was in terms of firepower. The gun itself is, of course, merely a
delivery system for the real weapon – the bullet. Therefore it is useful to
consider the characteristics of the ammunition used or, more specifically, its
'terminal ballistics'. An unexpected consequence of the introduction of small
calibre, high-velocity cartridges was a noticeable *decrease* in the lethality of
bullet wounds. The War Office's 1929 *Textbook of Small Arms* recalls that the
'.303 bullet with its diminished cross-section area and greater velocity had a
power of penetration which made its impact hard to feel in many cases, and its
track through the tissues was a clean puncture without circumferential damage
of any kind'. During the Russo-Japanese War it was reported that a soldier
marched twenty kilometres subsequent to being shot through the chest with a
Japanese 6.5mm bullet, 'and only experienced slight difficulty in breathing'.
After problems in stopping onrushing Pathan *Ghazi* on the North West
Frontier of India, the Indian Army developed Dum Dum bullets (taking their
name from the arsenal at which they were first produced) to overcome this
failing. The British Army subsequently issued hollow nosed rifle bullets to

achieve the same expansion upon impact. The Hague Convention of 1907 outlawed bullets of this type.

However, by the time of The Hague declaration, mainstream cartridge development was following an entirely different path. In 1898 the French had adopted a pointed bullet, with the Germans following suit in 1905. The intent was that the streamlining of the bullet would increase both range and accuracy. This proved to be the case, and pointed bullets subsequently became standard issue in most armies. The British armed forces adopted the Mark VII .303-inch cartridge, with pointed bullet, in 1911. However the so-called *spitzer* bullet had another characteristic. Because the centre of gravity is at the rear of such projectiles, they have an innate tendency to travel tail-first through the air. This tendency is held in check by the spin imparted to them by the rifling of the weapon from which they are fired. However, it is frequently the case that, on entering a human body, such a bullet begins to tumble end-over-end (or, to put it more accurately, turns around its lateral axis), causing far more damage to tissue and organs than would be achieved by a straight-travelling bullet and, arguably, worse than that caused by 'dum dums'.[13] Consider then the effect of such bullets, lethal out to ranges in excess of 3,000m and capable of remarkable feats of penetration. The British .303-inch bullet, when travelling at its maximum velocity, could penetrate one and half metres of clay, almost a metre of hardwood, or almost half a metre of sandbags. No helmet or body armour could withstand such concentrated kinetic energy. Furthermore a single bullet could easily kill or wound more than one man. Of the 'Great Powers' in 1914 Austria-Hungary was alone in not using such bullets as standard in its rifles and machine guns. It retained round-nosed bullets; as did Italy, who entered the war on the Allied side in May 1915.

A properly mounted and directed machine gun was the most effective way of delivering these deadly projectiles. It could do so in a number of ways. The tactic closest to the popular perception of a machine gun's use was 'traversing fire', which the French, with a grim appropriateness called *feu fauchant* – 'mowing fire'. To achieve this, the gun's elevation would be set to sweep an enemy parapet or area of advance and the gun would be traversed in the horizontal plane in between each burst of fire. The movie image of loosely mounted machine guns being swung rapidly around to hose the enemy ranks with fire is wholly inaccurate. Such shooting would be wasting not only ammunition, but also the machine gun's greatest asset – its precision. Machine guns are fired in bursts, the lengths of which vary according to the range or type of fire being conducted. Ten- to twenty-round bursts might suffice at ranges under 1,000 metres, while fifty-round bursts might be used at extreme ranges. In the British Army, 'rapid fire' was conducted at a rate of 250 rounds per minute. For this reason I have avoided listing the cyclic rates of fire of the various machine guns discussed in this book. They are a somewhat notional concept. First, because they can be varied – in recoil operated guns by adjusting the spring tension or using a recoil booster; in gas-operated guns by adjusting the gas port. Secondly, because machine guns are not used simply to discharge a continuous spray of bullets. As Longstaff and Atteridge trenchantly put it: 'The machine gun is fired to hit something, and is not to be handled as a mere destroyer of cartridges.'

Traversing fire would be conducted within a carefully defined arc – typically around 20 degrees – the movement of the gun within this arc sometimes being achieved by delivering a smart blow to one side or the other of the grips. This 'tapping' was particularly favoured by British machine-gunners, although it required careful adjustment of the clamp that controlled the traverse. Naturally, with the deflection and elevation mechanisms of the mount clamped tight, machine guns could fire on a fixed point or line, with minimal deviation, for as long as required. This type of fire was especially useful at night, with aim having been taken in daylight. As already noted, the effectiveness of machine gun fire was greatly enhanced by ensuring that the guns took the target in enfilade. Even on a straight frontage machine guns were most properly positioned on the flanks of the position, so as to afford them long diagonal lanes of fire across the front of the position, preferably with the opportunity of creating crossfire with other machine guns. It became standard practice, once a machine gun had been laid on a suitable line of fire, to select an aiming point up to 600m distant. If an enemy attack occurred, the gun was fired at this aiming point, as its operators could be certain that any men crossing their line of fire within that range would be exposing himself to the stream of bullets from their gun – for with the gun set for such a relatively short range, the trajectory of the bullets would not take them higher than head height.

When fired at longer ranges, the machine gun develops new capabilities. Not all bullets leaving a machine gun follow the same flight path. There is sufficient variation in their trajectories to create what is known as a 'cone of fire'. The area where the cone of fire intersects with the ground is known as the 'beaten zone' – an area typically elliptical in shape. The curving trajectory followed by bullets means that the beaten zone ellipse is shortened at extreme ranges, or when hitting upward sloping ground. Conversely it lengthens as the range lessens or if the ground of the target area slopes away from the firer. A British Vickers gun, firing at a range of 2,000m, onto flat terrain, produced a beaten zone 64m long by 6m wide. This characteristic of machine gun fire is not part of the popular perception of machine guns firing directly, at short ranges and on flat trajectories at advancing troops. What it gave machine guns was the ability to saturate areas of ground with fire and to deny the enemy safe access to chosen areas of the battlefield – even those out of view. Interlocking fire by a number of guns can be particular devastating as their beaten zones overlap.

The beaten zone can be extended by using what is known as 'searching fire' (*tiefenfeuer* in German). This involves small adjustments being made to the elevation mechanism on the gun mount between bursts, thus spraying the bullets over a wider area. The same effect can be achieved when more than one machine gun is firing by deliberately varying the elevation settings of individual mounts. This technique is known as firing with 'combined sights'. Searching fire has its origins in the very early days of machine-gunnery, when Hiram Maxim himself extemporized the technique at a trial of his gun in Switzerland. With his target barely visible, 1,200 metres distant, he adjusted his elevation up and down in order to guarantee enough hits to pass the test. Searching fire proved to be a most effective technique for maximizing the possibility of obtaining hits when the effects of fire could not be observed. It could also be used to deny the enemy safe access to large areas of ground. It is indicative of the technique's enduring importance that German machine gun mounts of the Second World War incorporated a special mechanism, the *Einstellring für Tiefenfeuer*, which automatically generated searching fire without the need for repeated manual adjustment of the elevation.

When these techniques and the capabilities of the ammunition are understood, it is easy to see the deadly potential of correctly handled machine guns in the open warfare of the early autumn of 1914. As we have seen, the most professional users of the weapon were the Germans, and their opponents – whether Russian or French – paid a hideous price in lives as a consequence. This slaughter was just part of the vast international hecatomb of 1914. Hopes of a quick decision based on manoeuvre were dashed. In part this was due to unrealistic strategic planning on the part of the various general staffs. On a tactical level it was found that all sides had gravely misjudged the balance between attack and defence. The generals had not gone to war unaware of the destructive power of modern weapons, but 'regarded defensive firepower as a costly obstacle that had to be overcome by a highly motivated attacker'.[14] Unfortunately they had failed to take into account three key developments that had altered the balance of firepower in favour of the defender. First and foremost was the development of quick-firing artillery; which is to say, guns with a recoil mechanism that obviated the need for them to be re-aimed after each shot. The First World War was the first conflict in which such weapons were to see anything like universal use. Secondly, developments in chemistry had led to the appearance of more powerful explosives. The proliferation of the machine gun was the final element of this triumvirate of death.

A new form of warfare

The tactics used by the attackers only served to enhance the danger posed by this unprecedented increase in defensive firepower. In the years preceding the war, the European Powers had striven to make ever-increasing numbers of men available for mobilization in the event of war. As a result, the armies that entrained for the front when the moment arrived included a high proportion of reservists and second-line troops. Tacticians worked on the assumption that these men would not be able to fight in the same dispersed formations as the Regulars, as they were both lacking in recent training and, it was presumed, more likely to go to ground under enemy fire if not kept in compact masses. The resulting use of dense formations combined with the increase in defensive firepower to exacerbate the hideous casualty list of 1914. Simply quoting large figures cannot begin to convey the shock and grief caused by such losses but, to pluck just two awful examples from many, 265,000 Frenchmen died in the first four months of the war and, in the East, Austria-Hungary lost 350,000 killed, wounded and captured during a mere four weeks, as a result of their ill-conceived Galician offensive.

A well-proven alternative to suffering heavy losses in open battle and one that had been utilized in many other wars, was to entrench. This implied a surrender of the attacking initiative, but by November 1914 the Western Front had begun to solidify into trench lines. This was perceived by all the combatants as a temporary measure; a mere interlude before a return to open warfare – *reculer pour mieux sauter*. Lieutenant Richardson of the Royal Welsh Fusiliers wrote, on 5 November, 'I am getting awfully bored by the trenches and feeling fearfully tired. I hope we won't be in them much longer. I wish they would order the advance.' He could be forgiven his lack of foresight. No previous war had become trench-bound to the same extent as the Western Front, nor did the other fronts of the First World War solidify to the same level of immobility. The unique character of the Western Front was the result of the simple equation of too many men and too many deadly modern weapons packed into too short a Front.

The role of machine guns in the creation of this situation is primarily evident in the skilled use to which the Germans put them during the opening months of the war. Admittedly, not all early attempts to use them offensively had been successful. During the first clash of the Russian and German Armies at Gumbinnen in East Prussia, German machine-gunners, who had boldly advanced to give direct support to an attack, were wiped out by Russian defensive fire; meanwhile the riflemen around them used their presence as an excuse to give up firing themselves and go to ground.[15] On the defensive, however, they showed from an early stage that they could be decisive. The historian of the

French 11th Infantry Division – the 'Iron Division' – recorded the fate of one of its regiments at the Battle of Morhange, in August 1914. Precipitated into a desperate counter-attack, they were caught in the fire of German machine gun batteries firing from flanking positions.

> Pettelat's battalion was the first to advance, as if on exercises. It was nailed to the ground by bursts of machine-gun fire and the fire of enemy howitzers which, from Hill 330, ploughed up with their murderous explosions the fields of oats in which our men lay spread. They were rivalled in heroism by their neighbours, the 2nd Battalion, whose commander had been killed at the start of the action, and who were decimated by the fire of machine guns from the wood of Kerperche, which broke their offensive spirit.[16]

Sir John French, commanding the British Expeditionary Force, recalled that during the so-called 'race to the sea' that autumn: 'From all parts of the line the same complaint came of the preponderance of the enemy's machine gun fire.' This German dominance was to continue once trench warfare had become established.

By the following summer, the German machine-gunners were indisputably shouldering the main burden of providing infantry defensive fire. To sustain this, new units of machine-gunners were created during 1915. Some regiments created additional machine gun companies. Additionally, numerous independent machine gun sections of three or four guns (*Feldmaschinengewehrzüge*, or *Maschinengewehr-Ergänzungzüge*) were created, to strengthen the most heavily engaged infantry units.[17] It is evident that German industry had to strain to produce enough Maxims to meet the new level of issue. The MG08 was produced by DWM and by the Prussian state arsenal in Berlin-Spandau. Immediate wholesale expansion of production was not found to be practical, although the German factories did have the advantage of starting from a substantial manufacturing base. A sufficient volume of production was not to be achieved until 1917. However, enough guns were produced in 1915–16 to fully equip at least those units engaged on the Western Front.

British intelligence reports following the Battle of Loos in September 1915 indicated that the German defences were almost entirely based around machine guns. A post-war German commentator identified the battle as 'the birthday of the idea of siting the heavy machine guns at the back of the position'.[18] David Lloyd George later wrote that his fervour for increasing machine gun production, while Minister of Munitions, was reinforced by his having seen photographs of 'dead Highlanders lying in swathes in front of a single German machine gun on the battlefield of Loos'. George Coppard, a British machine-gunner and author of the justly famous memoir *With a Machine Gun to Cambrai*, saw these same corpses as he went up to the line on 29 September:

> masses of British dead, struck down by machine gun and rifle fire. Shells from enemy field batteries had been pitching into the bodies, flinging some about into dreadful postures. Being mostly of High-land regiments, there was a fantastic display of colour from their kilts, glengarries and bonnets, and also from the bloody wounds on their bare limbs.

Most deadly was German machine gun fire against the British 21st and 24th Divisions as they attacked the German reserve line, on 26 September. With a splendid field of fire, and without being hindered by British artillery fire, the German machine-gunners opened up on the lines of advancing British infantry from a range of 1,500m. A historian of the German 26th Infantry Division recalled that 'Never had machine guns had such straightforward work to do, nor done it so effectively.'[19]

The great bloodletting of 1914, and the resulting struggle to develop tactics to cope with this new and unexpected form of warfare, had a marked effect on the status of the machine gun. First it became clear that field artillery was too vulnerable to counter-battery fire when deployed in a direct fire role. From now on, the norm would be for artillery to fire indirectly; thus placing more responsibility for the close support of the infantry on machine guns. Secondly, the losses suffered by all sides inevitably led to a reduction in the effectiveness of infantry rifle fire, as well-trained Regulars were replaced by Reservists and Volunteers. This was something felt especially acutely by Britain, which found its regular army, with its superb musketry skills, reduced to a small cadre. The obvious substitute for this loss was, as Major McMahon had pointed out, auto-matic firepower. Sadly McMahon had perished at Ypres, on 11 November 1914, while leading 4th Battalion Royal Fusiliers. Had he lived, he would have been pleased to see that the machine gun now began to occupy a very important place in the thinking of the highest echelons of the British military leadership. Within two weeks of McMahon's death, Baker-Carr had been charged with the creation of a BEF Machine Gun School in a French artillery barracks in St Omer (it was to move to a former convent in nearby Wisques in the following spring). Simultaneously, moves were afoot to increase the scale of issue of machine guns to the Expeditionary Force. The two guns per battalion were swiftly seen to be insufficient and it was decided to double their issue to four – this had been put into practice by early 1915. Plans were then made to redouble this figure as soon as production permitted – giving thirty-two guns per brigade. Importantly all new guns were to be of a new type, the Vickers, which had been approved for service in 1912. Only 109 of these had been in Army hands at the outbreak of war.

The Vickers gun

The Vickers gun and its ancillaries were to prove an astonishingly successful weapon-system, remaining in service with the British Army until 1968. The gun itself had its origins in a commercially produced 'Light Pattern' Vickers-Maxim gun, first produced in 1908 (the Maxim name was dropped in 1911). Vickers engineers, under the guidance of the firm's Chief Ordnance Engineer, George Buckham, conceived the modifications. The most significant change was that the whole action of the weapon was turned upside-down, so that the toggle now 'broke' upwards, into what had previously been wasted space in the upper part of the receiver, behind the feed block. This meant that the receiver could be reduced in depth. At the same time the Maxim's heavy brass water-jacket was replaced with one made of thin steel, longitudinally corrugated to add strength. These two developments greatly lightened the overall weight of the gun. The other important modifications were to the lock. The Vickers lock could be stripped in the field, permitting the swift replacement of broken parts – the firing pin for instance. It was also easily adjusted for 'headspace'. Head-space is the distance between the face of a firearm's lock or bolt and the point at which the cartridge rests in the chamber (i.e. rimmed cartridges like the British .303-inch round, headspace from the rim, whereas rimless cartridges, such as the German 7.92 × 54mm, headspace from the cartridge neck). The precise adjustment of this distance is crucial to the smooth operation of firearms, par-ticularly recoil operated weapons like the Vickers or Maxim.

Another feature of the Vickers was that spent cartridges were ejected directly through the bottom of the receiver, which was left open for the pur-pose (although covered by a shutter when the gun was not in use). The spent case was simply knocked free of the extractor by the underside of the barrel as the lock came into battery. This pleasingly simple system raised some qualms when the gun was first tested, as it was feared that the open receiver would encourage the ingress of dirt. In fact the reverse was true, as any foreign body within the weapon would generally drop out as it was fired. This was not true of the original Maxim design, which sometimes failed to deposit spent cart-ridge cases in the ejector tube. German machine-gunners were provided with a pair of tongs specifically for removing spent cases from the bottom of the receiver. Finally, a recoil booster device was fitted to the muzzle of the Vickers, to increase the cyclic rate of fire.[20]

The Vickers weighed just over 18kg and its tripod 22.7kg. By comparison the MG08 weighed over 26kg; the *schlitten* mount a massive 31.75kg. The Vickers tripod offered a good compromise between stability and ease of use. An expert crew could have its gun set up and firing within thirty seconds. In action the Vickers displayed a level of reliability which few automatic firearms have ever matched, inspiring great loyalty among all who used it in its fifty-five-year service career. George Coppard recalled his feelings on being selected for the machine gun section of the 6th Royal West Surrey Regiment: 'The Vickers .303 water-cooled gun was a wonderful weapon . . . Devotion to the gun became the most important thing in my life for the rest of my army career.' It is interesting to conjecture why the Germans attempted no serious redesign of the Maxim. In fact the advances made by Vickers were well known in Germany, as Vickers had a commercial relationship with DWM, Germany's largest firearms manufacturing concern. Undoubtedly the Army's commitment to the MG08 and the substantial numbers of that gun which were in service by the time news of the Vickers modifications reached Germany were a powerful disincentive to changing horses in midstream. The only Vickers-inspired element to find its way into German use was a recoil booster, which made its appearance in 1915. DWM did in fact place a lightened Maxim, known as the MG09, on the commercial market. While not using Vickers's inverted toggle, it did feature a strippable lock, adjustable for headspace, and a recoil booster. This weapon did not see German Army issue, although it served on both sides during the war, with the armies of Turkey, Serbia, Bulgaria and Romania.

Procurement and production

Since the 1930s controversy has raged among memoirists and historians of the First World War in Britain, regarding the speed and volume of Vickers gun issue to the British Army. This was ignited by Baker-Carr's book and by Basil Liddell Hart's *The Real War*, both of which appeared in 1930. Three years later the flames were vigorously stoked by the appearance of the David Lloyd George's *War Memoirs*. In them the former wartime Minister of Munitions and, subsequently, Prime Minister, excoriated the War Office and the British generals for their indifference to what he called 'the most lethal weapon of the war'. He based his claims on a report of what was evidently a rather testy confrontation between Sir Eric Geddes, Deputy Director of Supply, and the Secretary of State for War, Lord Kitchener, and also on what he alleged was the inadequate number of guns which the latter military potentate had ordered for the Army. To deal with the second point first, Lloyd George laments: 'How completely the military direction failed to appreciate the important part this arm would play in the War is shown by the fact that between August 1914 and June 1915 four contracts only were placed by them with Messrs. Vickers for a total of 1792 machine guns.' A Ministry of Munitions document dating from early December 1915 makes plain that, as with so many of Lloyd George's assertions, this was by no means the whole truth.[21]

The document in question is a report to King George V, himself apparently 'an advocate, before the war, of a greatly increased number of machine guns per Battalion', on the 'Machine Gun Position'. The same figure of 1,792 guns is quoted but, interestingly, the phrase 'continuation options existed' is appended. Still more fascinatingly, the original draft of the memorandum has been preserved alongside the copy sent to the King. This contains a footnote that quotes a statement from Kitchener to the effect that the 'continuation options' would in fact have facilitated the delivery of *27,000* Vickers guns to the army by the end of 1916. This whole footnote has been 'blue-pencilled' by an unknown hand. Given the fact that the document was to be shown to the King in person, it is not difficult to imagine that the editor was the Minister of Munitions himself. Thus we can discern the early groundwork for what was to become the Lloyd George machine gun proposition: that the weapon was underrated, and that production and orders were minimal until his advent. If, as a by-product, the generals – whom he so despised – were made to look incompetent, so much the better.

The other prong of Lloyd George's attack was Kitchener's response to a request from Geddes for a statement of the army's machine gun requirements. According to Lloyd George's version of this conversation, the Secretary for War exclaimed: 'Do you think I am God Almighty that I can tell you what is wanted nine months ahead?' He then asserted that he wanted as many as could be supplied. When Geddes pressed for an actual figure he 'said that the pro- portion was to be two per battalion as a minimum, four as a maximum and anything above four was a luxury'. Lloyd George revelled in recording his sub- sequent instructions to Geddes to 'Take Kitchener's maximum ... square it, multiply that result by two; and when you are in sight of that, double it again for good luck. This calculation gave thirty-two machineguns per battalion with another thirty-two for a margin.' (How a battalion was to find men to crew all these guns is not made clear.) One is not surprised at the nature of the con- frontation between the autocratic soldier Kitchener and the businessman Geddes, who had been plucked from the world of commerce by Lloyd George himself. However, once again, there is something missing from this version of events; namely the actual level of machine gun production at the time.

In fact both Kitchener's proposed 27,000 guns and Lloyd George's corn- ucopian vision were just so much pie in the sky – as both men were undoubtedly all too aware. In 1915 manufacture of the Vickers was limited to the Vickers plant at Erith, on the south-eastern outskirts of London. Peacetime production there was less than fifty guns *per year*. Strenuous efforts were of course made to expand production once war was declared. Unfortunately this expansion was circumscribed by the limited size of the factory and shortages of skilled labour. Between the outbreak of war and the end of 1915 just 2,772 Vickers guns had been produced there. Consequently, more than four guns per battalion would have been a luxury indeed! After the creation of the Ministry of Munitions, efforts to increase production were redoubled (and here Lloyd George can certainly take some credit). With the aid of government funds the Erith factory was expanded and a new Vickers plant was created at nearby Crayford. In addition an outside contractor was engaged to produce locks for the guns – the manufacture of which had been a bottleneck in production. Attempts were also made to have 6,000 Vickers guns produced in the USA and to create a National Machine Gun Factory. These latter plans never came to fruition however, and all British Vickers guns were produced by Vickers Ltd, at Erith or Crayford. By the end of 1916 wartime production totalled 10,260 – an impressive improvement on pre-war figures, but still woefully short of the requirements of the army and the goals set by the Minister of Munitions.

It is in this context that the bad-tempered exchange between Kitchener and Geddes should be seen. Hew Strachan has summed up the situation as follows:

> The criticisms of the army for its failure to use more machine guns were singularly ill directed when Vickers had managed to manufacture only 1,022 of the 1,792 due for delivery by July 1915. More contracts for more machine guns would not have added to the firepower of the army when industry could not cope with its existing orders. Piling contract on top of contract did not in itself create the plant or provide the labour necessary for production.

In fact, *in common with all other armies of the period*, the British Army made full use of as many machine guns as it could get its hands on. Despite Lloyd George's post-war scorn and Baker-Carr's lament that 'It took our General Staff many months of terrible loss to realize the worth of the machine gun'; it is clear that, from November 1914 at the latest, the army was fully aware of the need for more machine guns and machine-gunners – as attested by the creation of the Machine Gun School and the decision to double the scale of issue of machine guns. Only production difficulties prevented the required quantity of guns from being seen in the field until early in the following year. Incidentally, the increased level of issue initially had the effect of denying guns to the

Territorial and New Army formations which were undergoing training in Britain.

The French were slower than the British to react to the German machine gun superiority. There was a slow rise in production of the M1907, but this took until March 1915 to reach 200 guns per month, rising to 500 in the following August. The benefits of attempts to expand production were not truly felt until January 1916, when monthly output reached 1,000 for the first time. More significantly the pressures of war forced the French Army to look again at the Hotchkiss machine gun. The latest Hotchkiss gun was a far superior weapon to the St Etienne, and was adopted for service as the Model 1914. Initially it was issued to reserve formations only, but from 1916 its manufacture was prioritized. It was not to be until the spring of 1917, however, that production of the Hotchkiss began to exceed that of the obsolescent M1907. Thus, in contrast to information contained in most English-language books, the M1907 remained the most common machine gun in French service until late in 1917.[22] Incidentally the French also ordered 2,000 Vickers guns from Britain. They were permitted to do this, despite British shortages, as the filling of this small contract was used as a 'running-up' exercise for the new Crayford factory. As it happened the guns arrived too late for issue to the French Army and most were used by the French Air Service.

1915: evolution

The French Army was not, however, entirely blind to the superiority of German machine gun tactics. In March 1915 it was decided to group the existing machine gun sections into regimental machine gun companies, each disposing of eight guns. Additionally attempts were made to create brigade machine gun companies, although this development was hampered by the snail's pace at which new guns trickled out of the state arsenals.[23]

Similar moves were afoot in the British Army, where the tactical imperatives of the Western Front encouraged the *ad hoc* grouping of machine gun sections under brigade command. The unique British regimental system, wherein the battalions of a regiment did not serve alongside each other, but were attached to various brigades, precluded the creation of regimental machine gun companies on the German or French model. Therefore the brigade was the level at which the new organization was established. As early as May 1915, the 'brigading' of guns had attracted the favourable attention of the Chief of the Imperial General Staff himself.[24] By the late summer the arrangement had taken on an official character, with each brigade having its own machine gun company. The blow of losing organic machine gun support was softened for battalion commanders by the first appearance of the 'Lewis Automatic Machine Gun' at the Front. This light machine gun will be covered with the thoroughness its importance merits in a later chapter. At present it is sufficient to note that, from the second half of 1915, increasing numbers of this weapon were issued to British infantry battalions.

As well as tactical flexibility, the new system was found to simplify the supply and training of the machine-gunners. Other advantages were noted by an officer serving at the Front at the time: 'It allowed better control and co-ordination, more economical distribution and sounder dispositions in the brigade area than had been formerly the case with four independent sections. It also allowed worn-out sections to get out of the battle zone to be properly rested, a most important point.'[25] This last point was emphasized by another officer of the period, who later wrote: 'there was little relief for machine gun sections in the spring and summer of 1915 . . . Frequently an infantry battalion would be relieved and go back to billets, while its machine gun section was left behind in the trenches with another battalion of the same brigade.'[26]

The BEF Machine Gun School was now beginning to turn out suitably trained personnel. Moreover, those who survived of the pre-war machine gun experts were beginning to establish themselves in positions of influence. From March 1915, another Hythe man and proponent of machine guns, Captain George Lindsay, joined Baker-Carr at the Machine Gun School. Together they extended the remit of the school to include the teaching of machine gun tactics. Meanwhile, fellow enthusiasts were putting their theories into practice in the field. On 12 March 1915, at the Battle of Neuve-Chapelle, a Gurkha officer, Captain John Lodwick, won a DSO for marshalling the previously un-heard of number of twenty machine guns to beat off a massed German counter-attack. He had personally reconnoitred the newly captured area on which he deployed the guns, in order to site them to best effect. Hutchinson points out that Lodwick[27] had been an instructor in the Indian School of Musketry and the regimental history of the 3rd Gurkha Rifles names him as 'an acknowledged authority' on machine guns. The history of the Indian Corps in France and the regimental history both make specific mention of the fact that Lodwick was the brigade machine gun officer of the Garhwal Brigade; showing that the Indian Army was in the forefront of establishing the new model of machine gun organization.

Another representative of the British Empire in arms, the Canadian Corps, was also in the vanguard of developments in machine gun tactics. Serving within its ranks was one of the leading machine gun advocates of the day, French-born Raymond Brutinel, who, more or less on his own initiative, created a motorized machine gun brigade, mounted in armoured trucks. This unit accompanied the Canadian Expeditionary Force to England, but was not to be deployed in France until 1916. Nevertheless Brutinel himself did get to the Front. As will be seen in succeeding chapters, he was to prove a most influential figure in his chosen field.

Within the British Army itself a number of promising developments in machine-gunnery occurred in 1915. At Loos, where the German machine-gunners caused such devastation, 9th (Scottish) Division sent four Vickers guns into the attack with each of its battalions, but retained fourteen for use as a single battery to provide covering fire by day and to harass the enemy by night.[28] A few days later, on the same battlefield, George Coppard recalled firing at night in response to a distress signal: 'Although in the darkness we could see nothing, we had laid the Vickers on the enemy parapet at dusk, which ensured effective fire in the right quarter.' They were told that their 500 round shoot had cut up a body of German infantry attempting to reinforce a night attack.

The potentially close-quarter nature of trench warfare naturally exposed machine-gunners of all sides to the danger of attack by enemy infantry. To counter such attacks the British introduced the 'swinging traverse'. This involved loosening the traverse mechanism on the tripod sufficiently to allow the gun to fire while swinging slowly through an arc. It should be noted, how-ever, that this process was still far removed from the Hollywood image of machine gun shooting. The MG08 *schlitten* did not permit such a broad traverse. Instead the Germans ensured that their machine gun posts were plentifully supplied with hand grenades.

Also during 1915, Motor Machine Gun Batteries were created, deploying Vickers guns mounted on motorcycle combinations. Naturally they were un-able to fulfil a mobile role in trench warfare, but it should be remembered that trench warfare was viewed as a temporary phenomenon, so it was necessary to have mobile forces in being pending the expected return to mobile warfare. Despite these progressive steps, the official Army line on the machine gun showed surprisingly little change. Certainly more instructional material was available to machine-gunners than previously, but a training pamphlet issued in early 1916, which might be considered to encapsulate lessons learnt during the previous year's fighting, still contained the following admonition:

> Only in exceptional circumstances should machine guns open fire at long ranges; normally they will withhold their fire in order to obtain surprise effect. At ranges up to 800 yards well directed machine gun fire is annihilating in its effect. A very high standard of fire discipline and fire control is necessary to obtain good effect at longer ranges.[29]

Compare this with German pre-war instructions that fire should be conducted at ranges in excess of 800 metres if possible! Significantly the machine gun was still characterized as being 'to a great extent' a 'weapon of opportunity'. However, by the time this pamphlet was printed, a dramatic change had taken place within the British Army – a change that would transform the status and role of the machine gun, and raise its use to previously unheard of levels of sophistication.

Chapter 3

The Little Gunners

The distinguishing feature of modern Machine Gunnery is its offensive power.

(British General Staff Training Manual SS192)

On 22 October 1915 a Royal Warrant sanctioned the creation of a new corps within the British Army: the Machine Gun Corps (MGC). This was a remarkable and unique development. From this point onwards all of the Army's Vickers guns came under the control of the MGC. How then, did such a radical new scheme of organization suggest itself to the War Office and the Generals? Baker-Carr would have us believe that it resulted from a memorandum drawn up by himself and Captain Lindsay, in which they proposed the creation of an independent corps of machine-gunners 'whose personnel would be composed of selected men whose training would be complete and uniform and whose employment in battle would not be at the whim of a commanding officer, enthusiastic perhaps, but hopelessly inexperienced in the first principles of machine gun tactics' (one wonders if this was the *precise* form of words with which they attempted to woo the support of their superiors!). It would probably be closer to the truth to suggest that this document merely added weight to an argument that had already been won, *de facto*, by developments on the field of battle.

Baker-Carr and Lindsay could not have composed their memorandum until some time after the arrival of the latter at Wisques in March 1915. To suggest that such a document, produced by relatively junior officers, could result in the creation of an entirely new arm of service (for such was the MGC) within six months is nonsensical. However, it might well have helped to confirm the determination of the High Command to act. The War Office was in fact giving official recognition to advances that had already been made in the organization of machine guns in the field. As previously detailed, the exigencies of deploying machine guns effectively in action had necessitated the creation of a company structure – a development which may, at least partially, have been suggested by the experimental grouping of a brigade's machine guns which had taken place in 1910. However, there was an unfortunate side effect in that it became difficult to arrange personnel-related matters such as promotion, seniority and replacement. The machine gun companies were, in the words of Colonel Hutchinson, 'nobody's child'. The creation of the Machine Gun Corps can be seen fundamentally, therefore, as a rationalization of a situation that had arisen as a result of tactical requirements. It was facilitated by the arrival on the scene of the Lewis gun, which meant that the creation of the new unit would not deny the infantry an organic element of automatic firepower. In addition, the new corps would ensure the training of sufficient quantities of machine-gunners to man the large numbers of Vickers guns already scheduled for production. This point was certainly not lost on Lloyd George who, somewhat exceeding his ministerial remit, exerted pressure to ensure that enough recruits were allocated.[1] A Machine Gun Training Centre was created at the MGC depot at Grantham in Lincolnshire. Lindsay was plucked from the BEF school in France to establish it. Separate depots were created for the cavalry element of the MGC (at Uckfield in Sussex) and the Motor Machine Gun Corps (at Bisley in Surrey). Thus the decision to create the MGC was a pragmatic one. Few at the time can have envisaged the tremendous changes that would be wrought in British machine-gunnery as a consequence.

A *corps d'elite*?

The inception of the MGC did not pass without controversy. To an army founded on loyalty to 'the cap-badge', the severing of regimental ties to join a new-fangled unit was not always achieved without tears – at least in the case of officers. It is clear that, initially, sections forming the new MGC companies tended to keep themselves at a distance from one another – maintaining the personal links that they had forged as members of battalion machine gun sections. This situation naturally altered as new recruits diluted the original composition of the companies, but many deplored the separation of the machine-gunners from the infantry. Captain Dunn of the Royal Welsh Fusiliers (not himself a machine-gunner, needless to say) denounced it as 'This insane act'. Major R M Wright, a machine gun officer in the Guard's Division was later to suggest that 'Mutual confidence began to dwindle, and this lack of that complete understanding and sympathy, which can only come from friendship and intimacy, had a gradual but marked effect on the relations between the machine-gunners and the infantry, increasing the difficulties of securing perfect co-operation between them.'[2] This complaint, patently uninfluenced by any anti-MGC bias, was evidently heartfelt. Sadly for Major Wright, the formation of the MGC was a decision taken in response to pressing tactical and administrative requirements, which brooked no opposition from those who might wish that the Army could remain the close-knit 'family' that it had been prior to 1915.

The MGC developed its own *esprit de corps* with surprising rapidity. George Coppard became a member of the MGC after serving as battalion machine-gunner in a proud county regiment, but recalled that:

> It was exciting to feel that we were no longer in a small unit, subject to the whims and dictates of every infantry officer and NCO. From then on, as members of a specialised corps, we came under the orders of our own superiors. Carried down the scale, this meant that an unpaid lance-corporal in charge of a gun in action, who became detached from his own superiors, would be the sole judge as to the best position for his gun, and when and where it should be fired.

He was later to reflect that 'It was not a great regiment with glamour and what not, but a great fighting corps, born for war only, and not for parades.'

The 'Emma Gees' (from the phonetic rendering of the alphabet used in telephonic communication at the time), or 'Little Gunners' as they were some-times known, eventually came to regard themselves as an elite unit. A more darkly humorous name they adopted for themselves was 'The Suicide Club' – a soubriquet which, although not exclusive to the MGC, was undoubtedly merited due to the fact that machine-gunners were customarily the prime target for enemy mortars and field guns and, in the course of withdrawals or retreats, were frequently obliged to sacrifice themselves as rearguards. Paddy Griffith[3] has questioned this self-assumed status, on the grounds that units obliged to provide drafts for the MGC were hardly likely to send their best men. This is true up to a point, but it ignores two important factors. First, at its inception, the corps was composed of the existing machine-gunners of infantry regiments who, given the demands of their trade, were likely to have been selected from among the fittest and most intelligent members of those regi-ments. Secondly, the MGC was not obliged to accept those it considered to be below the required standard. Arthur Russell, author of two memoirs of his time in the corps, recalled that unfit men were immediately weeded out of the ranks of new drafts upon arrival at Grantham.[4] The MGC in fact insisted that new entrants must be:

a. Intelligent & well supplied with common sense.
b. Fairly well educated.
c. Of good physique. Strong, healthy & able to carry heavy loads over bad ground while keeping pace with infantry.
d. Mechanically inclined & of a logical turn of mind.
e. Possessed of plenty of 'guts', be resolute, brave & well discip-lined as at times M.G.s have to be deliberately sacrificed e.g. rearguard or other desperate situation.[5]

The level of physical fitness required is graphically illustrated by the standards laid down for the machine-gunners of the Canadian Expeditionary Force (CEF). Members of Canadian gun teams (of three men – teams were actually of six, but three were reserves) were expected to be capable of going into action immediately after 'doubling' 600 yards, carrying between them the gun (15kg), tripod (22.7kg) and two 250 round belt boxes (over 10kg each). The founders of the new corps also went to the lengths of drafting in an officer and some sergeants from the Guards to ensure the highest possible levels of drill and turnout. As one MGC officer recalled: 'I have seen officers with two medals on them doing right-hand salute, left-hand salute, all around that drill field, and going on doing it until they could do it like a Guardsman.'[6] Doubtless these unfortunate officers would have echoed the veteran George Coppard's view that the NCOs at Grantham were 'a bunch of blow hards'.

If any problem did exist with the aptitude of personnel assigned to the MGC, it was, as Colonel Hutchinson himself noted, most likely to stem from the selection of officers for the new corps – 'it did not occur to anyone that the machine gun officer, whatever his other qualifications, must be a ready mathematician, possess an instinct for map-reading, and have a mechanical bent'. In the final analysis, the elite or not-elite argument is probably not worth pursuing. The important thing is the way in which a unit regards *itself*. If, like the MGC, it *considers itself* an elite, this is likely to be reflected in its battlefield performance. This was certainly the case with regard to the Machine Gun Corps.

The formation of the MGC took several months over the winter of 1915–16. The scale of the achievement was implicit in the size of the new corps: 4,000 officers and 80,000 men. The 'Big Push' on the Somme was destined to be its first real test as a unit. In the mean time the training and equipment of machine-gunners developed apace. In the spring of 1916 the BEF machine gun school moved to an hotel at Camiers on the Channel coast – here training was carried out among the sand dunes and along the beaches (the latter useful for experiments where observation or analysis of the fall of shot was necessary). Training for the Lewis gun was, from this point, separately conducted at nearby Le Touquet. Baker-Carr himself did not tarry long by the seaside, but moved on to devote his abundant energies to an even more novel weapon system – the tank – and thus swims out of our ken. Major J H Luxford, a New Zealand machine gun officer, was impressed by the progressive regime that prevailed at Camiers, where 'any idea that might assist in the development of the uses of the machine gun was thoroughly probed and tried, and if it proved to be good no stone was left unturned to secure its introduction'.[7] Aside from such experimentation, the gunners of the MGC were trained to a high degree of efficiency in their basic tasks. Coppard noted that the winners of a competition for fastest team into action were able to set up their gun and knock down a steel plate at 200 yards range in just twenty-seven seconds. Russell gives details of realistic training conducted at Grantham for the crucial business of taking over machine gun positions at night.

British equipment

The Vickers gun itself had, by this time, acquired a variety of accessories, both official and unofficial – some of more utility than others. A Barr and Stroud range-finder, of the type used by the artillery, was issued to each two-gun section. However Arthur Russell notes that it was seldom of use because the enemy was either too close to make it worthwhile, or completely out of sight. A former Emma Gee told me that he only once saw this device in use – an activity swiftly curtailed by the death of the officer employing it. Russell was however delighted to be designated as the section range-finder, for it entitled him to carry a Smith and Wesson revolver, rather than encumber himself with a rifle. (It was not until 1917 that rifles were completely replaced by revolvers as the personal armament of all machine-gunners.)

A small auxiliary tripod was produced for emergency use. It can be seen in numerous photographs of the era, folded up under the water-jacket, to which it was clamped. George Coppard recalled one being used to surprise a German working party by firing from no man's land by night. However, another witness derided the device as 'useless' due to the heavy vibration of the gun when fired from it – a fellow officer failed to hit a group of Germans at 600 yards range when using one.[8] A number of attempts were made to create flash hiders for use during night firing. These tended to be of a tubular configuration, but some are reported to have had a tendency to trap unburnt gases, which were liable to explode with an enormous flash at inopportune moments. Experimentation with such devices, and growing use of aiming aids (see below), did not pass without amused comment from at least some machine-gunners. The December 1916 edition of the MGC magazine contains a cartoon depiction of the 'Gun, Vickers, .303″ Mark X' – a weapon almost unrecognizable under a welter of accessories – with the admonitory caption: 'A warning to gadget merchants.'

Vickers gunners were inculcated with knowledge of the many idiosyncrasies of their weapon, and the specialized maintenance routine necessary to keep it in peak condition. Barrels became worn and inaccurate after 15,000–18,000 rounds had been fired and required changing. The complicated lock was vulnerable to dirt and freezing. It was common practice for one of the team to keep a clean lock in his pocket for immediate insertion into the gun if serious action was anticipated. During icy winter nights, locks would be removed regularly and replaced with warm ones. The other great danger to the smooth operation of the gun was the swelling of the fabric ammunition belts due to wet conditions. Ammunition boxes were waterproof, but the belt still saw a great deal of unavoidable exposure to the elements. During the Third Battle of Ypres, it was found necessary to build rainproof reloading stations for the MGC to operate their belt-filling machines in. In 1915 it was discovered that the Vickers suffered ammunition feed problems in the wake of exposure to poison gas. Baker-Carr himself diagnosed the cause, after gamely donning a respirator to spend hours firing a Vickers in a gas-filled room. The chlorine gas reacted with the brass cartridge cases to form a verdegris-like deposit on them. Thereafter, ammunition boxes were gas-proofed.

New methods of fire

On a tactical level, the most important effect of the creation of the MGC was the gradual adoption of new methods of fire, which took advantage of the unique characteristics of machine gun fire. The curved trajectory followed by the bullets, and the precision and predictability which was afforded by the use of a firm mount, permitted machine guns to conduct two types of long-range fire that were denied to other small arms. First, they were capable of being fired over the heads of friendly troops. Naturally this had long been undertaken where guns could be fired at, or from, some topographical eminence. It had been done in the Russo-Japanese War and the British had used the same technique even earlier, on the North West Frontier of India. However, the natural trajectory of bullets, coupled with the fact that the elevation of the machine gun could be precisely set and controlled, enabled overhead fire to be conducted on completely flat terrain. The range would be taken, and mathematical calculations made to work out the minimum elevation setting commensurate with the safety of intervening friendly troops. The elevation was then set by placing a clinometer on the body of the gun. It was vitally important that guns firing overhead were firmly mounted, and that there was no chance of the tripod sinking into the ground, even fractionally. Barrels that had fired more than 12,000 (or, for preference, 8,000) rounds were not used in guns firing overhead. Wooden stakes or cross-bars might be used to prevent over-zealous gunners from traversing, elevating or depressing their weapon outside safe parameters. Later, special stops, fulfilling the same function, were extemporized for the tripod. The workshops of Second Army are recorded as producing quantities of these in the spring of 1917. Obviously, firing from the flank would usually obviate the need for these elaborate procedures, as well as subjecting the enemy to enfilade fire. However, the trench lines of the Western Front seldom offered the opportunity to take up flanking positions – at least until they were broken into in the course of attacks – so overhead fire became a much-used technique. The Guards Division made a notable early use of it at the Battle of Loos, against Hill 70.

Naturally the experience of friendly small arms fire passing over one's head took some adjusting to. The noise, which could be heard as a crack, a rush of wind, or a hum, was unnerving, as all accounts agree that it made the bursts of fire sound much closer than they actually were. The actual clearance specified was 11 yards at 100 yards range, rising to 40 yards at 1,500 yards and 80 yards at 2,000 yards. Sadly officers of infantry battalions did not have the facility to try the ruse employed by the Royal West African Frontier Force officer quoted by Goldsmith. Wishing to demonstrate the efficacy and safety of overhead fire to his men, he arranged to fire over them from 300 yards at a target just 800 yards distant, placing his wife in the trench with them, to 'give them confidence'.[9] On the Western Front, even when the technique became commonplace, inexperienced troops could still be unsettled by it. Dunn recorded such an instance occurring as late as 1918:

> Men of D Company who were questioned said the machine-gun barrage upset them. It is doubtful if they had been told of it. It seemed to be only three or four feet over their heads, and its curious swish caused most uncomfortable feelings; they felt as if they were stepping out of the deep trench into a stream of our own bullets, and they did not like the idea of being shot from behind.

Overall however, it seems clear that, as Major Luxford put it, the infantry 'learned to welcome the sound of the familiar crackle immediately an SOS signal was sent up'.

The Germans frequently took advantage of topographical features to fire safely over the heads of their own troops. They were of course aided in this by the fact that they normally held the advantage of the ground. Being on occupied territory they could exercise greater freedom than the Allies in setting up their defence lines – conducting planned withdrawals to prepared positions where necessary. However, they did not attempt overhead fire on level ground until late in the war. Indeed, this practice was expressly forbidden in an instructional publication written by German machine-gunnery expert Friedrich von Merkatz in 1915:

> Our own troops can be fired over with entire safety since the sled with its aiming apparatus permits of the certain control of the machine-gun sheaf [i.e. cone of fire]. In a flat country, firing over the heads of the firing line is barred on account of the flatness of

the trajectory. Theoretically, it would be practicable to fire over the heads of our troops without danger at the longer ranges on account of the height of the trajectory, but the line of sight would always be directed at our own troops or pass very slightly above them, so that such shooting is out of the question.[10]

The second important new method of exploiting the fire-characteristics of machine guns was the use of indirect fire – i.e. the use of machine guns as small artillery pieces, engaging targets that were not visible to the gunners. The theory behind this technique had long been understood. At the instigation of Lieutenant Parker, the US Army had conducted experiments with it (albeit unsuccessfully) as early as 1908. More sustained research, and the mathematical work required to provide a reliable basis for the conduct of such fire, was carried out by a group of British enthusiasts at the Hythe musketry school. However, it was 1915 before such fire was successfully carried out in the field. Captain Wright dates its adoption for general use to the winter of 1915–16, calling it the 'type of fire . . . long advocated by machine-gun experts, "cranks" to their enemies, "enthusiasts" to their friends'.

To conduct such fire the proposed target would be located on a map, and the position of the machine gun relative to it would be determined with ruler and protractor. It is, of course, no accident that the first use of this technique in the field coincided with the production of accurate maps of the Front.[11] Calculations would be made to determine the gun's potential cone of fire and the trajectory of its bullets (an important consideration if firing over the head of friendly troops). A clinometer, combined with the graduated elevation dial fitted to the tripod, would be employed to set the gun to the correct elevation (the dial was replaced by a simpler and more intuitive wheel in 1918). From 1915 onwards, the tripod was also fitted with a direction dial at the base of the crosshead. As per overhead fire, it was necessary to ensure that the gun was firmly emplaced (generally by placing sandbags on the tripod legs) and unable to sink into the ground. Aiming posts would be driven into the ground, enabling the gunner to change swiftly between different pre-selected target areas (for night shooting, shaded lamps might be employed to provide aiming marks). Such changes would be made either in conformity with a timetable, or in response to prearranged SOS signals from the infantry (the standard SOS signal at this time was a red flare). Initially the effectiveness of such fire was wholly reliant upon the expertise and dedication of the officer responsible for setting up the guns. By 1917 however, the training centre at Grantham had produced specialized graphs and slide-rules for use in setting up indirect fire, as the technique had, by this time become central to the tactics of the MGC.

Austro-Hungarian machine-gunners were also versed in the techniques of indirect and overhead fire – possibly this was the fruit of their early experimentation at Bruck. It was to remain enshrined in their tactical instructions until 1918, although Austrian machine gun officers captured by the British in Italy asserted that, although they had been trained in these techniques, none, by this stage of the war, were using them in the field.

Indirect fire was used to harass the enemy, and to deny him safe access to areas of 'dead ground'. It was not introduced without a certain amount of controversy. Baker-Carr himself was not enamoured of the tactic. While he reigned supreme at the BEF Machine Gun School, the technique was recommended for searching roads and approaches by night 'a most efficient and disconcerting form of "Hate" if properly employed and regarded, mainly, as a side show', but he disagreed with commanders who had machine guns 'diverted from their proper uses and converted into "Pocket Howitzers"'. Captain Dunn was moved to complain that 'The command and position of these weapons had been removed yet farther from the front; less and less were they available for direct and opportune fire, and more were they practised on hypothetical targets on the map; it was not unknown in those days for hundredweights of lead to be buried in some intervening bank or elevation.' Proponents of indirect fire were nevertheless bolstered in their enthusiasm for it by three factors. First, the fact the small arms ammunition was relatively cheap, and available in huge quantities. Secondly, work had to be found for the machine guns which found front-line positions increasingly untenable due to the ever-increasing weight of artillery and mortar fire that they attracted. Thirdly they quoted the statements of German prisoners who had endured such fire. Various limitations on the effectiveness of indirect fire are scrupulously noted in a British machine gun training pamphlet of May 1917, but 'In spite of these limitations, indirect fire, according to information of prisoners and deserters, has caused a considerable amount of moral and material effect on the enemy.'[12] Ernst Jünger, in his famous memoir *Storm of Steel* recalled being on the receiving end of indirect harassing fire on the Somme: 'We were especially irritated by one machine-gunner who sprayed his bullets at such an angle that they came down vertically, with acceleration produced by sheer gravity. There was absolutely no point in trying to duck behind walls.'[13] His shaky grasp of ballistics does not conceal his dislike of the sensation.

British machine guns on the Somme
It was during the Battle of the Somme that many of the advances in machine-gunnery that were being pioneered by the MGC began to be put into practice. Christopher Duffy's invaluable study of the battle through German eyes

rightly notes that 'the combat on the Somme is associated so strongly with the carnage wrought by the German machine-gunners that it is possible to over-look the fact that the British had machine guns as well, and were using them in novel and effective ways'.[14] Sadly, progress was not universal. The MGC did not benefit from operating under its own commanders beyond company level – at least when in action. The deployment of machine guns for battle was a matter decided by the staff of brigades, and could vary according to their knowledge of the new tactics, or the influence (wielded without the backing of authority) of the commander of the Brigade Machine Gun Company. As a consequence, particularly early in the battle, many machine guns and their crews were sacrificed in misguided attempts to advance with the leading waves of infantry. Burdened with guns, tripods and ammunition boxes, they made tempting targets for their German counterparts. Furthermore, the sending of machine-gunners into an advance on foot was a sure-fire way of wasting their firepower – for only limited amounts of ammunition could be carried: certainly only a fraction of the quantity generally carried with each gun.

When not in action Vickers guns were carried on limbers. These comprised a pair of two-wheeled vehicles linked together, which were drawn by four horses or mules. Each two-gun section had one 'Fighting Limber', which carried their guns, plus 9,000 rounds of ammunition (7,000 rounds of it in belts). In addition, each two-section platoon was served by a 'Number 3 Limber', which carried an additional 14,000 rounds and two belt-loading machines. Should the terrain be impassable for limbers, mules with pack-saddles could carry single guns; but this was avoided if possible, due to the limited amount of ammunition that could be carried. MGC officers were encouraged to take their Fighting Limbers as close as possible to their gun positions, as long as they did not draw enemy fire upon the guns themselves. Thus prolonged manual portage of ammunition was to be avoided if at all possible.

As the Battle of the Somme pursued its bloody course, there are signs that wiser counsel began to prevail in the employment of machine guns. A case in point is the intelligent use of machine guns in the assault on Delville Wood by 2nd Division, on 27 July 1916. The gun teams of 99th Machine Gun Company were not sent forward with the first wave of the attack, but moved up with a supporting battalion (1st Royal Berkshire Regiment). Infantrymen were seconded to the machine-gunners to carry ammunition and water, enabling a reserve of trained gunners to be maintained. In addition, each gun team was accompanied by at least one selected rifleman, to protect it against enemy snipers. It can't be claimed that this form of deployment aided the actual capture of the ground (the huge weight of supporting artillery fire was the main reason). However, once the far edge of the wood had been reached, the relatively intact MG Company, 'boldly handled', in the words of the Official History, led the way in repelling the inevitable German counter-attacks. At nightfall the infantry, with the exception of 400 men with twelve Lewis guns, were withdrawn, whereupon responsibility for defence of the wood devolved largely upon the Machine Gun Company. This enlightened use of machine guns was in fact no coincidence, as the Brigade Major of 99th Brigade at this time was none other than George Lindsay, who had been posted to the Western Front after his stint at Grantham.

Indirect fire also began to play an increasingly important role. As at Loos, the 9th (Scottish) Division led the way. On 14 July, its 27th Brigade mounted an assault on the village of Longueval. Four of the 27th Machine Gun Company's guns were kept out of the attack and used in an indirect fire role; being sited two kilometres away, outside Montauban. This was making full use of the Vickers gun's ability to lay down accurate long-range fire. The defenders of Longueval were subsequently to complain of suffering from the fire of these guns. On the afternoon of the same day, an episode that has since entered the mythology of the battle took place, when two regiments of cavalry – the 7th Dragoon Guards and the 20th Deccan Horse – advanced between High Wood and Delville Wood. Subsequent highly coloured recollections of eyewitnesses have painted a ghastly picture of cavalrymen and horses being slaughtered by German machine guns as they attempted to charge into the woods. A J P Taylor roused himself to new heights of mordant eloquence to describe it: 'The British infantry saw a sight unique on the Western Front; cavalry riding into action through the waving corn with bugles blowing and lances glittering. The glorious vision crumbled into slaughter as the German machine guns opened fire.'[15] In fact the cavalry made a relatively successful advance across open ground, through a gap between two battalions of the German 26th Infantry Regiment, before dismounting and forming a defensive line. They suffered very few casualties. German sources, as revealed by Christopher Duffy, indicate that a major reason for the low loss rate among the cavalry was the effectiveness of British machine gun fire – particularly against the 3rd Garde Division, as it moved up to support the 26th Infantry Regiment. Thus we are simultaneously provided with a good example of the growing effectiveness of British machine-gunnery and a warning against too easily accepting the time-worn vision of British troops continually wasting their lives in the face of German machine gun fire.

George Coppard recalled firing indirectly in support of the Australians at Thiepval on 12 August 1916. His recollections were detailed and are, I feel, worth quoting at length here; giving, as they do, so complete a picture of the process:

> The position of my gun would enable its fire to enfilade the ground between the new German front line and the support trenches, at a point where the attack was to be made that night. Sixteen thousand rounds had to be fired ... Clinometer calculations were made by an officer, and at early dusk Nobby and I crept out to a shell hole at the back of the parados and mounted the gun, to which we had fitted a new barrel ... At zero plus fifteen minutes I opened fire and, with the aid of a shaded light and two pre-set pegs, kept the fire in its correct elevation and scope of traverse ... Number three was crawling to and fro, building up the supply of ammo. The rest of the team were in the dugout, filling the empty belts by a hand-operated machine. Periodically fresh water was added to the cooling jacket, and a touch of oil was applied to the sensitive parts of the gun with a brush kept in one of the grip handles. Although it was dark we could see and feel what we were doing without difficulty. The ammo, British cordite type [as opposed to American-made ammunition, which used a different propellant; less suited to the Vickers], gave little trouble. Now and then a stoppage occurred, but the position of the crank handle quickly indicated the necessary clearance action.
>
> Various signal flares lit the sky but were of no significance to us, as our firing had to continue until stand-to. Our job was to assist in pinning the enemy down in his support trenches, and to harass any reinforcements coming forward. There was also a sunken road likely to be used, which had to receive our attention. I kept up the fire, and, as expected, a whizz-bang battery began to search for us. Clark and I were apprehensive, although not exactly displeased, as we guessed our fire was damaging in some way. If the German infantry asked for assistance from their light artillery, it was on the cards that we were causing mischief.[16]

The machine gun barrage

The Somme battles also witnessed the first regular use of the machine gun 'barrage' – a tactic which was an amalgamation of overhead fire, indirect fire and the now well-proven technique of grouping guns. It was later officially defined as 'centrally controlled fire by a large number of guns on to definite lines or areas, in which each gun engages approximately 40 yards of frontage'. Raymond Brutinel subsequently claimed to have 'invented' the machine gun barrage. He certainly has a good claim to have fired the first barrage of the Great War – on 2 September 1915. However, it is quite evident that the machine gun experts of Britain and her other Dominions were simultaneously thinking along the same lines. In fact Brutinel was not well placed to conduct such experiments, as the Canadian Expeditionary Force was, at that time, equipped with a gun that was patently unsuitable for use in barrage fire: namely the Colt 'Potato Digger'. Between 1914 and 1916, 662 of these guns were purchased to equip the CEF, after it became clear that sufficient supplies of Maxims or Vickers guns would be unlikely to appear in the short term. In addition to the overheating problem outlined in the previous chapter, the Colt proved sadly unreliable in the field. It was prone to jamming by dust and mud and its extractor was notorious for breaking at crucial moments. Its maintenance required no less than 348 different spare parts and tools (compared with 123 for the Vickers). In the words of one Canadian veteran 'The Colt was a washout.'[17] In an attempt to make the gun more serviceable, the Canadians added a cable and pulley device to enable the gun to be cocked from the rear, rather than the front. They also fired it from Vickers tripods when possible. The latter became available in quantity before the guns themselves. The CEF Machine Gun Companies did not completely replace their Colts with Vickers guns until late 1916. The Canadians remained at the forefront of machine gun barrage fire development, but Brutinel's later claim that the British wallowed in blissful ignorance of barrage fire until after April 1917 is nonsense.

There are in fact examples of the successful use of machine gun barrages by the British during the Somme battles. Undoubtedly the most famous instance was that of a barrage conducted by 100th Machine Gun Company in support of an attack on High Wood on 24 August 1916. The officer responsible was Captain G S Hutchinson, who later recorded it in detail. Rapid fire by ten guns was maintained continuously for twelve hours. At the end of this period they had fired 900,750 rounds. Two companies of infantry had been deputed to stockpile vast quantities of ammunition and water, although a failure in the supply of the latter necessitated the requisitioning of the contents of 'the company's water bottles, and all the urine tins from the neighbourhood'. The target was the area behind the crest-line on which High Wood stands, through which German infantry attempting to counter-attack had to pass. According to a German prisoner, the effect of the machine gun fire was 'annihilating'.[18]

Hutchinson's barrage was actually much out of the ordinary, both in terms of its duration and in the lavish expenditure of ammunition. A more conventional barrage is used as an example of 'Emergency Indirect Fire' in the syllabus of work for the officers' course conducted at Grantham. In an action at Ovillers, three sections of a machine gun company fired barrages which forestalled a German counter-attack from Pozières. The date given is 14 July, but the positions shown on the accompanying map are more suggestive of 16 or 17 July – which would suggest that the machine-gunners were attached to 48th Division. The company had already registered the positions of its guns in relation to Ovillers church and, on receipt of a warning from a reconnaissance aircraft, three barrages were fired within twelve minutes at the German assembly area, which lay in 'dead ground' behind Pozières (all too literally in one case, which took in Pozières cemetery). The divisional commander 'considered that the Machine Guns had checked the attack by their own unaided barrage'. Arthur Russell recalled firing a company barrage at Morval on 25 September: 'In spite of the thunder of our artillery, the humming of thousands of bullets fired from eight of the 13th Company's machine guns could be heard as they whizzed over our heads on their way to make an impassable barrier between the enemies reserves and his hard pressed front line troops.'[19]

The effectiveness of these tactics in 1916 was enhanced by the defensive tactics of the German Army, which made a positive fetish of attempting to recapture lost positions by immediate counter-attack. This policy inevitably exposed large bodies of German infantry to the fire of the increasingly effective Royal Artillery and to machine gun barrage fire. Herein lay the origins of the vicious and sanguinary nature of the Somme battles. As John Terraine wrote: 'The picture of the British infantry rising from their trenches to be mown down is only a true picture of the battle of the Somme when set beside that of German infantry rising from their trenches to be mown down.' Importantly for the British, the machine gun barrage was a tactic well suited to the offensive operations which the strategic situation impelled them to prosecute. The British instructional pamphlet SS192, which first appeared in 1917, was a distillation of lessons learnt on the Somme. It boldly claimed that:

> The distinguishing feature of modern Machine Gunnery is its offensive power. The offensive intention has always been present, but lack of training and technical equipment hindered its realization and led to the impression that the Machine Gun, whilst a powerful weapon in the defence of ground gained, could do little to assist the attacking troops in its capture.
>
> Modern machine gunnery has reversed this passive tendency ...

Consequently, from late 1916 onwards barrage fire became central to the activities of the MGC. This was not a policy pursued without controversy.

First it is evident that many infantry officers simply lacked any under-standing of the techniques used by their MGC counterparts. Robert Graves, in *Goodbye to All That*, appeared to think that machine-gunners, conducting what to him appeared indiscriminate fire, were attempting to boil water for tea! As George Coppard politely commented: 'tea laced with mineral oil would be pretty ghastly. Also the machine gun crews who fire "indiscriminately" might well be engaged on barrage fire, and infantry officers would not necessarily be aware of that fact.' In the Canadian Corps, Brutinel fought a running battle with artillery officers who doubted the value of machine gun fire against un-observed targets. In May 1917, we find Captain Dunn in fine sardonic vein with regard to a barrage fired during the attack on Tunnel Trench in the Hindenburg Line: 'Anyhow, long before this the Machine-Gun Corps claimed to have broken up the concentration, laying out 1,500 Germans – with the jawbone of an ass, according to common opinion.'

Even within the MGC, there were those who remained a little sceptical. Major Wright of the Guards Machine Gun Regiment accepted that the technique was 'excellent in theory' but notes some difficulties. First the all-pervading First World War problem of communications – it was difficult to maintain sufficient contact between the machine gun batteries and those they were tasked to support. Secondly there was the difficulty of observing the effects. Thirdly, climactic and barometric conditions could affect the behaviour of bullets in flight. Wright stated that 'calculations were seldom made and only rough allowances made for these disturbing influences'. Having said this, he admits that the beaten zone produced by a machine gun meant that absolute accuracy was not essential. He also noted that

> any form of covering fire is valuable. It has a moral effect upon the enemy's troops, and tends to keep their heads down, even if it does not inflict casualties. Also they cannot watch it and avoid it, as can be sometimes done by intelligent observation of an artillery barrage. The new tactics did at any rate give machine-gun companies a definite supporting role in an attack, when the ground was unfavour-able for the use of direct covering fire. In fact, indirect covering fire is better than none.[20]

Others were more wholehearted in their enthusiasm for barrage fire. Lindsay, writing in December 1917, stated that the infantry 'once they are assured by experience that it is safe, acclaim and ask for indirect over-head fire'.[21] Tellingly, by February 1918, the formerly mocking Dunn was confiding the following hope to his diary, with regard to the enemy: 'Pray he may not copy our machine-gun barrage: he has copied our Stokes mortar action.'

The Germans and French in 1916

While the British experimented with 'scientific' machine-gunnery, the Germans were becoming all the more wedded to a system of defence based around the direct fire of machine guns. Their experiences are reflected in an order concerning machine guns promulgated in the 6th Bavarian Infantry Division:

> The Battle of the Somme has again shown the decisive value of machine guns in the defence. If they can be kept in a serviceable condition until the enemy's infantry attacks and are then brought up into the firing position in time, every attack must fail. The greater the efforts the enemy makes in the future to destroy our trenches before his assault by an increased expenditure of ammunition, the greater the extent to which we must rely upon the employment of machine guns for repulsing attacks.[22]

The critical importance of machine guns to German defensive tactics is shown by their readiness to blame defeats upon the failure of machine gun support. Army Group commander Crown Prince Rupprecht of Bavaria blamed the success of British attacks in September on the number of German machine guns buried in forward trenches by the bombardment. Duffy relates that the jamming of machine guns was noted as a factor in the temporary loss of the Butte de Warlencourt on 18 October. The orders of the 6th Bavarian Division forbad the exposure of guns in dangerous forward positions, stating that the majority should be emplaced behind the second or third trench line, with wide fields of fire, or the possibility of enfilade fire. The remainder of the guns were to be further back, in concealed pits or platforms hidden in trees. Machine guns were to be defended from close quarter attack by grenade armed infantry 'who can also work the gun if necessary'. Incidentally, this 'cross training' of infantry in basic machine-gunnery skills was attempted at one point in the Canadian Corps, but otherwise did not feature in the training of the BEF. The French attempted to ensure that their infantry NCOs, at least, were familiar with the basic workings of machine guns. Paradoxically a French pamphlet on how to work *enemy* machine guns, was eventually circulated in the BEF, under the title: *'I have captured a boche machine gun'* ... *WHAT CAN I DO WITH IT?*

A German appraisal of lessons learnt from the Battle of Verdun called for machine guns to be disposed 'chequer-wise' in depth to the rear of the first position and to be ready to open flanking fire on any enemy penetration of the system. Other analyses of the Somme fighting advocated the maintenance of unaimed 'horizontal barrage fire' (i.e. harassing fire) over dead ground or at night and the inclusion of some machine gun commanders in each counter-attack, so that newly recaptured areas could be surveyed swiftly for suitable machine gun positions. The Germans made no use of barrage fire in the British sense of the term at this time. The reason was simply that their existing tactics, and the flexibility that they enjoyed in choosing their positions, suited their defensive posture well. However some impetus was given to the development of machine gun tactics in the German Army by the creation, during 1916, of an elite group of machine gun marksmen (*Maschinengewehr-Scharfschützen*) who were to operate under the direct control of the High Command. Originally organized in six-gun companies, they were, by August 1916, grouped in three-company detachments (*Abteilungen*). Their initial purpose appears to have been to promote the use of machine guns in the attack. Consequently any division taking part in offensive operations could expect to have one of these detachments attached to it. Eventually all divisions holding front-line positions on the Western Front could expect to have the support of one of these *Abteilungen*.

The creation of such units was facilitated by a steady improvement in the availability of guns with which to equip them. During 1916 the German machine gun stock doubled from 8,000 to 16,000. Captured weapons were also used – notably Russian Maxims, many of which were rechambered to the German calibre (the British, incidentally, converted captured German Maxims, but on a much smaller scale). Regimental machine gun companies also benefited from the increased production. Initially some of them began to deploy twelve, or even as many as fifteen, guns. Subsequently, however, a rationalization took place, with each infantry battalion now being furnished with a six-gun company (Jäger, Assault and other autonomous battalions got two companies). To achieve this, the independent sections and detachments formed in 1915–16 were abolished. In direct contrast to British developments, this represented, according to one authority, a 'tendency, resulting from long combat experience, for the infantry and the machine guns to grow together'.[23] This highlights one of the key points concerning the use of machine guns in the Great War: that tactical and technical developments were common to all combatants, but differed in accordance with the type of war they wished to fight. For the British, the creation of the MGC was a logical response to their need for offensive machine-gunnery. For the Germans the maintenance of a strong organic element of machine gun firepower with their infantry was the choice best suited to their defensive tactics.

Up to the end of 1916, the French remained less reliant upon the machine gun than either of the other main combatants on the Western Front. Baker-Carr visited their machine gun school at Vincennes and found that little or no tactical training was given. He noted the 'curious fact that the French, right up to the end of the War, never thoroughly appreciated the value of the machine gun and placed far more reliance on their field guns for repelling German attacks'. Certainly there were notable instances of the *Soixante-Quinze* being employed successfully to beat off German attacks at Verdun; but it should be remembered that Baker-Carr's direct association with machine guns ceased during 1916, so his knowledge of later French developments was probably sketchy.

At the close of 1916 the French reviewed and revised their machine gun tactics. The most notable outcome was the recognition that the machine gun now provided the principal element of infantry firepower. The specific instructions for the employment of machine guns that emerged were, essentially, little more than an official compilation of common-sense tactical advice. In the attack, the machine guns were to apply their firepower to areas where the assault had been halted and, subsequently, to help consolidate the captured positions. They might also substitute for the artillery where speed or surprise was essential. In defence they were to be echeloned in depth, in protected emplacements, with a view to conducting enfilade fire on any attacker. The French developed one particularly useful defensive technique. Thin lines of barbed wire were stretched along the line of fire of emplaced machine guns. When enemy attackers met this wire and were held up, fire was opened – maximizing the effect of the enfilade. Naturally, German observers would be likely to attempt to follow such lines of wire to their associated machine gun emplacements, but the French learnt to either start the wire some way in front of the gun, or to let it run on to the rear of the emplacement.[24]

During 1916 a further reorganization of French machine guns had taken place. The fourth company of each infantry battalion was converted into an eight-gun machine gun company – giving a total of twenty-four guns per regiment. This move certainly signalled the ultimate realization that, on the modern battlefield, machine guns provided the core of infantry firepower, rather than an adjunct to it. The increasing numbers of machine guns that were becoming available sustained this dominance. Production of the Hotchkiss rose in 1916 from 450 per month in January to 1,200 in December. Meanwhile production of the M1907 hit its peak (1,900 guns) in the latter month. Thereafter manufacture of the former continued to expand, while that of the latter dwindled.

'Tommy and his Machine Gun'

Curiously, as the slaughter conducted via the medium of the machine gun reached new heights in the second half of 1916, the weapon itself managed to retain the positive image that it had earned prior to the war. In 1916 Arcadian China of Stoke on Trent produced a crested-china souvenir figurine depicting a Tommy hunched over a machine gun. Even as late as 1917, British machine guns were being reproduced in the form of souvenir china. A contemporary advert for Beecham's Powders used an image of a Tommy firing a Maxim gun, with the slogan: 'A Good "Maxim" To Remember. Beecham's Pills will keep you up to the mark.' The picture had, in fact, been drawn at the Front by Bruce Bairnsfather. He wrote that he drew it 'endeavouring to be cheerful whilst reclining in six inches of mud and water at the bottom of my dug-out'. There is no actual proof, but it seems probable that Bairnsfather's drawing was the inspiration for Arcadian China's 'Tommy and his Machine Gun'.

Another machine-gunner artist was Otto Dix, who, after originally joining the artillery, served for a large part of the war as a non-commissioned officer in a German Army machine gun unit. If for nothing else, he would commend himself to the attention of this book as the only artist ever to have executed a portrait of himself clutching a Maxim gun. Dix did not allow the war to interrupt his progression as an artist. He created apocalyptic gouache and pastel visions of the shattered landscape and strange light – natural and man-made – of the Front, and also monochrome drawings of an altogether darker nature. One of these, *Falling Ranks*, depicts men being cut down by machine gun fire. A visible arc of fire is depicted, almost geometric in form. The path of its traverse through the advancing rank of men can be traced by their attitudes – standing, stricken, falling or prostrate. After the war Dix established himself as a leading member of the *Neue Sachlichkeit* (New Objectivity) art movement and, in 1924, produced *Der Krieg*, a series of etchings that graphically reflected his wartime experiences. One of the prints was titled 'machine-gunners advancing'. It depicts a section of machine-gunners moving up to the line on the Somme. They are struggling down a steep slope, burdened with their heavy MG08s and boxes of ammunition. On closer inspection it can be perceived that the mud, in which they wade knee-deep, is replete with dead bodies. As the other prints in the series show, Dix pulled no punches in depicting the horrors of war, but one is tempted to question whether such a sea of corpses was not a piece of artistic licence. The answer is emphatically clear from the published recollection of a British machine-gunner, who endured just such a nightmarish march on the same battlefield:

> Corpses became more numerous as we approached the line. The stench, increasing in direct ratio to the number of corpses, seemed to have at least the solidity of corpses by the time we reached the shambles of the old front line trenches, full to overflowing with bodies some of which a matter of days, perhaps only hours or minutes ago, housed lives more valuable to the world than those of their slayers . . .

Fed up and far from home! I ask you? I got to the stage eventually
where if a handy corpse provided a better foothold than the sur-
rounding quagmire, I used it. I was not alone in that.[25]

That memoir did not see the light of day until the 1970s. Other contribu-
tions to the same volume hint at another crucial element of the machine-
gunner's experience – hatred of the enemy. The willingness, indeed eagerness,
of soldiers to kill their enemy has been 'Bowdlerized' from the popular myth of
the Great War – which tends to view the men of both sides as bound together
by the bonds of common suffering. Recent studies have undermined the universal applicability of such a vision.[26] The recollections of machine-gunners
certainly support this scepticism. One writer recollects being captured briefly
during 1918, along with some Gordon Highlanders: 'A Hun officer beat one of
the Gordons with a stick, and said he was going to shoot us machine gunners,
as we had inflicted heavy casualties on his men.' Shortly afterwards they are
rescued by some Riflemen and 'We told the K.R.R's of 37th Division about the
officer who had beaten the Gordon prisoner, and they bayonetted him.' A
willingness to shoot machine-gunners was not of course restricted to the
Germans. Lieutenant-Colonel C S Grafton, a Canadian MGC officer, recalled
with admiration that:

> The German machine gunner had invariably shown himself to be the
> pick of the enemy troops – fighting his gun to the bitter end. And it
> was usually the bitter end, for the qualities of mercy had been pretty
> well strained to breaking point by the time attacking troops had
> reached the source of so much of their trouble and from which
> flamed forth so much death in their ranks.

Arthur Russell's 1977 memoir recalled that 'At 4 o'clock this Christmas Day
[1917] afternoon my gun was due to fire five hundred rounds as a yuletide gift
to the Jerries over the way.' George Coppard had found himself in a similarly
unfestive mood on Christmas Eve 1915:

> I can categorically state that we were in no mood for any joviality
> with Jerry. In fact, after what we had been through since Loos, we
> hated his bloody guts. We were bent on his destruction at each and
> every opportunity for all the miseries and privations which were our
> lot. Our greatest wish was to be granted an enemy target worthy of
> our Vickers gun.

It is also instructive to note that the poet Wilfred Owen – in recent times seen
as the pre-eminent voice of the soldier as victim – won his Military Cross in the

Hindenburg Line in 1918 for seizing a captured machine gun and 'inflicting considerable losses on the enemy'.[27]

Thus the experience of the real 'Tommy and his machine gun' was far removed from the jolly public image still prevalent in 1916. Interestingly however, it was equally distant from today's popular perception of the experience of First World War soldiers. The modern British perception of these men tends to see them as 'victims' of the war – who, if left to their own devices, would have been happier playing football with the enemy in no man's land than fighting them. As the examples given above testify, the reality was more complex. The real man was as likely to be perpetrator as victim, and believed that he was right to be so. He took his duty seriously, and pleasure in carrying it out effectively. Machine-gunners had the added incentive of a desire to perfect their technical expertise. Little wonder, then, that the machine gun – as long as it was used in the service of what was overwhelmingly viewed as a just war, or even 'crusade' – should hold on to the favourable image that it had enjoyed in pre-war days.

Chapter 4

Walking Fire

> Company officers, in selecting men, should imagine that they have a
> new motor car and wish to choose one of their men to be trained as
> chauffeur. A Lewis gun is a more delicate piece of mechanism than a
> motor car and needs more constant attention.
>
> (British General Staff pamphlet SS122)

In the spring of 1912, two representatives of the Automatic Arms Company of
Buffalo, New York, sailed for Europe. Their intention was to generate sales of
and, if possible, establish production of a new weapon: the Lewis Automatic
Machine Gun. This was an air-cooled, gas-operated gun. Its inventor, Colonel
Isaac Newton Lewis, of the US Army, had developed it from a water-cooled
design that had been unsuccessfully promoted by a Dr Samuel McClean. The
failure of McClean's attempts to sell his gun had left his patents in the hands
of the Automatic Arms Company. Lewis, who had a proven track record as
an inventor of military technology, was brought in to convert the McClean gun
into a functional weapon.

The gun attracted some interest in British and continental military circles –
particularly with regard to its potential as an aircraft weapon. It was therefore decided to set up a new company to oversee its manufacture in Belgium.
Problems were encountered in acquiring production facilities there, but the
new company – Armes Automatiques Lewis – accepted an offer from the
Birmingham Small Arms Company (BSA) to manufacture the gun in England
under licence. By the autumn of 1913 work had commenced on the production
of a sample batch of fifty guns to be made in seven different calibres. Three of
them were made in British .303-inch calibre for evaluation by the Army and
Royal Navy, while five were produced in Belgian 7.65mm calibre for despatch
to the parent company. Alarmingly (in the light of subsequent developments) three guns chambered for the German 7.92mm cartridge were taken to
Germany by company representatives in July 1914. The deepening international crisis curtailed their visit however, and the Lewis sales team was
obliged to make a hasty exit, via Russia.

There can seldom have been a more timely business decision than that taken by the directors of BSA to set up manufacture of the Lewis gun. However, initial trials with the British armed forces did not result in its adoption for service. In all countries prior to the First World War, there was no conception of light machine guns or automatic rifles as a distinct type of automatic weapon. Machine guns were machine guns as far as the armies of 1914 were concerned. As a consequence, the Lewis was contrasted unfavourably with the new Vickers guns just entering service. In comparison with the Vickers it was indeed a frail thing, and could not produce the same sustained rate of fire. Therefore there appeared no good reason to adopt it. The coming of war was to change this state of affairs. Meanwhile, it was in the hands of the Belgian Army, rather than the British, that the new weapon was first to come to prominence. During the German invasion of Belgium in 1914 twenty Lewis guns were used – the five sent to Belgium in 1913, along with a further fifteen in British .303-inch calibre. The noise made by these guns (later described in a British training manual as 'unmistakeable') led the Germans to nickname the Lewis the 'Belgian Rattlesnake'.[1]

The British and the Lewis gun

The coming of war reawakened the interest of the War Office in the weapon, and a series of small orders was placed with BSA from 31 July onwards. The rapid expansion of the Army, coupled with the slowness of Vickers gun production, made any serviceable machine gun welcome. Unfortunately BSA could only manufacture the Lewis at a rate of ten per week at this time. However, acting on its own initiative, the company began, in the autumn of 1914, to build a completely new Lewis gun plant, with a capacity of 150 guns per week. This capacity was to be used to the full after the energetic Lloyd George, as Minister of Munitions, took control of procurement in May 1915.

While far from being as robust as the Vickers, the Lewis gun was certainly lighter; weighing in at 11.8kg (unloaded). It used the system of gas operation which, in future years, was to become the norm for weapons of its type. Gas tapped from the barrel was used to drive a piston positioned beneath the barrel. The movement of the piston was transferred to an operating rod, which unlocked the bolt. The latter turned in a fashion similar to a rifle bolt; the bolt-head having lugs which locked it at the moment of firing by engaging in recesses in the barrel. The bolt rode on a post projecting from the operating rod. The firing pin was also affixed to this post, and projected through the face of the bolt at the moment of firing. The return movement of the action was achieved by means of an unusual clock-like spring, which was tensioned by the rearward movement of the operating rod, via a rack and pinion mechanism.

The gun was fed from above, by a forty-seven round, rotating drum magazine. The unique feature of the Lewis was its cooling system. The barrel was surrounded by an aluminium 'radiator' featuring longitudinal fins. This was clad in a tubular casing that extended beyond the muzzle. Lewis intended that the muzzle blast would be harnessed to draw cool air through the casing (which was open at the rear) and over the radiator fins. The merits of this system have been much discussed. It is certainly possible to fire bursts from a Lewis with the whole cooling system removed. However, anything contrived to aid the cooling of air-cooled guns of this era would have been worth trying; and at least it kept the hot barrel away from the firer's hands.

The Lewis had many drawbacks. It was relatively fragile and its action was complex and prone to failure. A post-war manual lists fifteen potential stoppages.[2] An additional problem was posed by the method of ammunition feed. The drums or 'pans' were not easy to carry into action, and the fact that they were open at the bottom invited the ingress of mud and dust into the interior of the gun. As an air-cooled weapon fired from a light bipod, the Lewis could in no way compete with the Vickers in the delivery of controlled, sustained fire. After around 1,000 rounds of rapid fire, the Lewis would seize up and need to cool off for half an hour or more. Nevertheless on its own terms, as a light machine gun, it was inherently accurate. It was also vastly more portable and less conspicuous on the battlefield than a Vickers gun. Finally, and most importantly, it recommended itself by being immediately available and (as the war progressed) procurable in huge quantities. The steady trickle of guns delivered during 1915 (just over 2,000 by November of that year) expanded into a torrent as the Ministry of Munitions instructed BSA to prioritize Lewis production. By March 1916 800 guns per week were being manufactured – a figure which rose to 1,000 per week by the end of the year.

There is evidence that the Lewis did not immediately win the hearts of its users at the Front. This was the outcome of the fact that no doctrine specific to the use of 'automatic rifles' existed at the time. The Lewis was therefore seen as a markedly inferior machine gun: 'a very shoddy affair after the Vickers', as one officer put it.[3] Its reliability was (with some justification) questioned and its bulky pans of ammunition criticized. Behind the lines it proved an awkward handful. Vickers guns benefited from mule-drawn limbers as transport, whereas Lewis gunners were obliged to push a cart which, in the words of Brigadier Jack, 'resembles a coffin (suitable for containing the body of their designer) mounted on two strong bicycle wheels with solid rubber tyres. It is so low set that the men hauling and pushing them must crouch. Each of our carts used to be towed by a pack mule ... But this labour-saving practice has recently been disallowed.' From the beginning of 1917 this unpopular contraption was dropped in favour of carrying the guns and ammunition on general service wagons.[4] The reliability and ammunition problems were not so easy to overcome. In September 1918 we find Brutinel writing a memorandum advocating its replacement with a shoulder-fired automatic rifle, to be issued on a basis of four guns per platoon.

Despite its drawbacks, however, it was not long before the Lewis had found favour at all levels of the British Expeditionary Force and, for proof, we must turn once again to the Ministry of Munitions machine gun memorandum[5] of December 1915. This notes that 'within the last ten days' (the memo was drafted on 11 December) GHQ in France had requested that the allocation of machine guns in the field should be increased to sixty-four guns per brigade (sixteen per battalion), with half of these being Lewis guns. Thus, one of Sir John French's last acts as Commander of the BEF was a most progressive one. As in the case of the Vickers gun, production levels initially proved unable to sustain the proposed scale of issue.

GHQ's figure of eight Lewises per battalion appears generally to have been achieved by late 1915, although of course, at the same time, the battalions lost their integral complement of Vickers guns. By the summer of 1916 infantry battalions on the Western Front deployed between eight and sixteen Lewis guns. The figure of sixteen guns, which had certainly become the norm during the following year, permitted the issue of one Lewis to each platoon. By this time, four further guns were on issue to battalion HQs for the purpose of air defence. Further growth in production of the Lewis finally allowed the issue of two guns per platoon during 1918. In little more than three years therefore, a sea-change in infantry weapons technology within the British Army had been effected. The tactics to accompany the new technology followed in close succession. Beginning in March 1916, a succession of training pamphlets addressed the question of the correct use of the Lewis. The first of these, *Notes on the Tactical Employment of Machine Guns and Lewis Guns*, devoted just three pages to the new weapon. It made clear the status of the Lewis as 'a supplement to, and not a substitute for the machine gun. However, apart some wishful thinking about what might be done with Lewis guns in a return to open warfare it limited itself to suggesting that the Lewis should be used to cover sections of the line that could not be swept by Vickers fire, and warned against carrying it forward in the first wave of attack. In common with so many British tactical developments, it was the Battle of the Somme that provided the impetus for the creation of a more sophisticated rubric for the employment of the Lewis gun.

Even as the battle progressed, more thought was being given to the tactical potential of the 'automatic rifle'. The pamphlet SS122, published in September 1916, specifically identifies the knocking out of machine guns as the 'special job' of Lewis guns. It also suggests that the Lewis should be handled 'as a sailor handles a submarine ... popping up unexpectedly, delivering a crushing blow ... trusting to escape by their mobility and invisibility to some other unexpected place from which they can repeat the dose'. After the elapse of sufficient time to analyse the Somme battles, further and more concrete instructions (this time eschewing nautical metaphors) appeared in *Instructions for the Training of Platoons in Offensive Action* and *The Normal Formation for the Attack* (SS143 and SS144, February 1917). These placed the Lewis gun at the heart of a new platoon organization – for now at last there were sufficient guns to provide one for every platoon. The platoon was now to be composed of four specialized sections – riflemen, bombers (i.e. grenade throwers), rifle bombers and a Lewis gun section comprising the two gunners with six riflemen (who helped carry the magazines). The platoon could advance in two lines – in which case the Lewis section advanced behind the bombers, on the most exposed flank – or in dispersed 'artillery' formation – in which instance the Lewis section marched at the rear of a loose 'diamond'; ready to deploy to either flank. When the platoon met resistance, the first task of the Lewis gunners was to cover the deployment of the other sections. Thereafter it was to work around the flank of the enemy position to cut their line of retreat.[6] This, at least, was the theory. The memorandum of September 1918, written by Brutinel, suggested that the amount of mechanical and technical knowledge that it was necessary to impart to Lewis gunners reduced the amount of time that could be allotted to training them in tactics. One man's opinion, no doubt; but not, given its origins, a criticism to be dismissed out of hand.

Thus the platoon (rather than the company, as had been the case in 1914) became the principal fighting formation of the infantry. Its chief element of firepower was now provided by the Lewis gun: a happy circumstance at a time when many officers were complaining that they could no longer expect accurate musketry from their men at any range greater than 200 yards. The addition of Lewis guns and rifle-grenades to the platoon's armoury permitted it to deal unaided with a variety of threats. This concept was strongly driven home in the 1918 instructions for the *Tactical Employment of the Lewis Gun,*[7] which included a whole section on 'Co-operation', which not only encourages co-operation between the different elements of the platoon, but also exhorts company commanders to collaborate with the commanders of any light trench-mortars and Vickers guns in the vicinity. Much stress is also laid on the correct use of the Lewis in open warfare. Emphasis is placed on the potential of platoons, through the correct integration of the Lewis, bombing and rifle sections, to act effectively alone. Indeed it goes so far as to state that 'The reduction of a small strong point, which may be garrisoned by a few riflemen or a single machine gun, gives a platoon commander an opportunity for exercising his tactical skill.' One important aspect of the recommended techniques is the use of the Lewis in enveloping movements. This is seen as particularly useful when attacking a defended wood or village. It is worth noting here the curious fact that these instructions could remain unknown to such a dedicated officer as Colonel Hutchinson, who complained that 'No clear instructions had ever been issued on the subject' (of the respective roles of the Vickers and the Lewis) and that 'no publication seems to have appeared defining the tactical employment of two different weapons whose mechanisms alone superficially suggested the similarity'. None of the pamphlets noted above can have found their way to him – doubtless because he was a machine-gunner and not an infantryman. This is indicative of the danger of presuming that the publication of manuals automatically resulted in the universal adoption of new tactics. It is also worth bearing in mind when reading criticisms of machine gun use by infantrymen or artillerymen who would not have seen instructional material relevant to machine-gunnery.

The cavalry were not equipped with the Lewis. Instead it was decided to issue them with the 'Hotchkiss Portable Gun' – which was in fact almost identical to the Benét-Mercié 'machine rifle' used by the US Army. Hotchkiss could not meet simultaneous French and British demands for this weapon (the French wanted it for their air service) as well as the French Army's requirements for their Model 1914 machine gun. Consequently they decided to concentrate on the manufacture of the machine gun at their Paris factory, while creating a new factory in Coventry to make the 'portable' gun. Manufacture commenced in May 1915 and, by the Armistice, 40,000 of the 'Hotchkiss machine gun Mark I' had entered British service.

The 'Chauchat'

Apart from Russia, whose cavalry had successfully employed the Madsen gun as early as 1904, other nations had been at one with Britain in not perceiving a separate role for a light machine gun. Their responses after the outbreak of war were diverse. As noted in Chapter 2, the hasty development of the French M1886 rifle meant that its only truly modern feature was its ability to fire the new smokeless ammunition. As soon as other countries developed rifles to compete with it, its obsolescence became abundantly clear. As a consequence the French decided that they would once again steal a march on their ancestral foes, the Germans, by developing a self-loading rifle, chambered for a new high-velocity cartridge. Several designs were secretly developed, along with ammunition of striking modernity.[8] Unfortunately, war intervened before a rifle could be issued.

Hence it was primarily with the bolt-action rifle and bayonet that the French infantry strove to repel the invader in 1914; subsequently proceeding to sustain many more thousands of casualties attempting to drive him from their soil in the spring offensives of 1915. During the course of the latter campaign, the desirability of some form of automatic firepower which could be carried into the attack became clear. Fortunately – concurrently with their experimentation with self-loaders – the French had also looked into the concept of a fully automatic rifle, or Fusil Mitrailleur (FM). One of these, designed by Colonel Henri Chauchat and Charles Sutter, had reached a fairly advanced stage of development by 1914. Thus an indigenous design was available for production. This was just as well, because it proved impossible to modify the Lewis gun to accept the French 8mm service ammunition.

On 28 April 1915 the commander-in-chief General Joffre (invested with powers that his counterpart Sir John French could only dream of) demanded the immediate manufacture of 50,000 Chauchat-Sutter machine rifles, with deliveries to commence in November.[9] In an attempt to achieve this, production facilities were sourced at the Gladiator motorbike and cycle factory in Paris. With the aid of the factory's production manager, Paul Ribeyrolles, the CS rifle was modified to facilitate mass production, and became known as the CSRG – the latter initials denoting Ribeyrolles and Gladiator. Not surprisingly, Joffre's imperious demands could not be met. Difficulties in tooling up delayed production, which did not commence until the spring of 1916. By September, however, almost 26,000 had been manufactured and had entered service as the Fusil Mitrailleur Modèle 1915.

Although sharing the same official designation as the Lewis, the CSRG was a very different breed of 'automatic rifle'. Chauchat and Sutter had based their weapon on the 'long-recoil' system of operation first patented by John M Browning in 1900, for use in shotguns and rifles. In long-recoil the recoil energy is harnessed to drive the barrel and bolt rearwards for a distance equivalent to the whole length of a cartridge. Once this movement has been completed, a spring returns the barrel to battery. In the course of this return movement, the bolt-head turns to unlock itself from the breech. As bolt and barrel separate, the spent cartridge case is ejected. Finally the bolt is released and, under the pressure of another spring, moves forward to chamber and fire a new round. This system of operation is relatively straightforward, but liable to seize up in combat conditions, due to the variety and quantity of surfaces moving against each other. The ingress of dust or mud is always likely to cause excessive friction. Overheating was another potential problem if sustained fire was attempted. Six to eight round bursts were laid down as the norm for the CSRG.[10] One further weakness of the CSRG was the awkward positioning of the housing for the recoil spring, which projected over the butt. This obliged the firer to take up a somewhat odd firing position, or risk a bruising blow to the cheek.

The distinctly unlovely looking CSRG has acquired a dreadful post-war reputation for unreliability, despite the fact that it served the French Army well in the most difficult of circumstances. This disparaging attitude would appear to stem from a number of sources: the parochial attitude of Anglophone firearms experts; a tendency to judge it against more modern light machine guns, rather than in the context of early automatic rifle technology; and the rough and ready appearance of the CSRG itself. The latter was, of course, of little account in wartime; rates of production were what mattered. To this end a second manufacturer – Forges et Acieries de la Marine à Hommecourt – commenced production in September 1917. Eventually, over one quarter of a million CSRGs were built: making it the most numerous automatic weapon of the First World War.

The CSRG was used in small quantities at Verdun, but the first full issue (at a level of eight guns per company) was to the infantry of Sixth Army, in preparation for their role in the Battle of the Somme. Initially the CSRG team consisted of just two men, but the difficulty of carrying sufficient ammunition soon saw this raised; first to three, then – in the autumn of 1917 – to four. The new weapon had a similar effect to the Lewis on the platoon structure of the army to which it was issued. During 1916 the infantry *Section* (platoon) was divided into two *Demi-Sections*. The first comprised a squad of grenadiers and a squad of two CSRG teams. The second comprised two squads of riflemen (*Voltigeur*), each supported by two rifle grenadiers. Significantly the personnel of the second *Demi-Section* could (within reason) be called upon to keep the first *Demi-Section* up to strength.[11] In September 1917 a further reorganization was made, in response to combat experience. The CSRG teams were now grouped with the rifle grenadiers and operated in cooperation with specialist *Voltigeur* and Grenadier squads.[12]

The German machine gun was the Chauchat's principal prey. The development of the complementary squads within the *Section* facilitated the stalking and destruction of enemy machine gun emplacements or pill boxes. The CSRG could also be used to provide suppressive fire in the course of an advance. Its teams were trained to provide 'walking fire'; with the gunner firing from the hip while advancing, while his loader (the *Pourvoyeur*) walked alongside and changed the magazines, so as to maintain an unbroken sequence of bursts. The lightness of the CSRG lent itself to this sort of use in a way that

1. Sir Hiram Maxim.

2. The Maxim system. This drawing shows the action locked (above) and fully open (below). The operation of the 'toggle' mechanism is clear. The cartridge 'floating' above the barrel represents the one held in the feed block. Beneath the barrel is the ejector tube. (See pp. 12–13.)

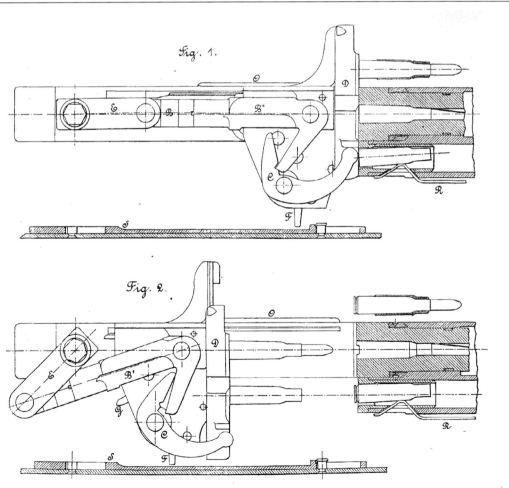

Fig. 1.

Fig. 2.

Section of Lock, Closed and Open, of German Maxim R.C.A.M.Gun.

3. The smokeless powder revolution.
Left: a Russian 10.67mm black powder cartridge.
Right: a Russian 7.62mm cartridge with smokeless propellant.

4. Part of a sign advertising Vaux 'Maxim Ale'.

. The German MG08, fitted with an optical sight and an armoured cover for its water-jacket.
(Taylor Library)

. Postcard showing French soldiers demonstrating AA fire with the M1907 machine gun.

7. Austro-Hungarian
troops with Schwarzlose
Machine Guns; making
a show of readiness
against air attack.
(*Photograph courtesy of the
Imperial War Museum, London,
Neg. no. Q 56997*)

8. Italian machine
gunners with a Revelli
gun. (*Photograph courtesy of
the Imperial War Museum,
London, Neg. no. Q 54778*)

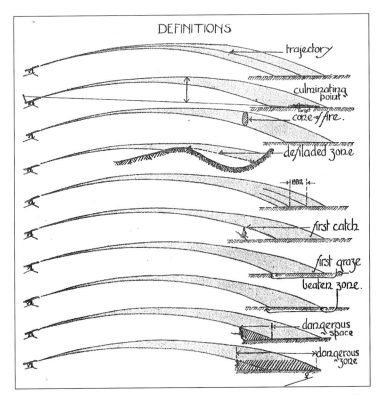

DEFINITIONS

trajectory

culminating point

cone of fire

defiladed zone

EBZ

first catch

first graze

beaten zone

dangerous space

dangerous zone

9. A graphic representation of machine gun cones of fire and beaten zones. Taken from British machine gun training notes. (See pp. 41–2.)

10. The Vickers gun. Empty petrol cans were frequently used to condense the steam from the water-jacket. (*Taylor Library*)

11. Vickers gunners in action on the Somme. The gun is well dug in, with its tripod legs covered with sandbags and earth. The rear sight appears to be set for a range of 2,200 yards. The auxiliary tripod is folded up under the water-jacket. (*Photograph courtesy of the Imperial War Museum, London, Neg. no. Q 3995*)

12. Emergency Indirect Fire. Taken from British machine gun training notes, this diagram shows barrages fired by three sections of a machine gun company at the assembly area for a German counter-attack at Pozières. (See pp. 67–8.)

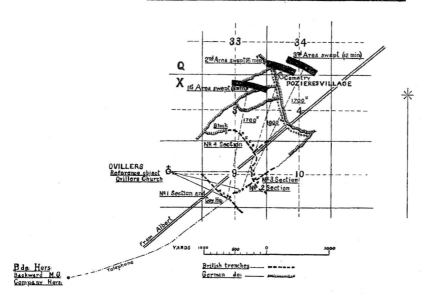

EMERGENCY INDIRECT FIRE.

13. Advertisement for Beecham's Pills, with artwork by machine-gunner Bruce Bairnsfather.

14. German machine-gunners advance, in an etching from Otto Dix's Der Krieg cycle of prints.

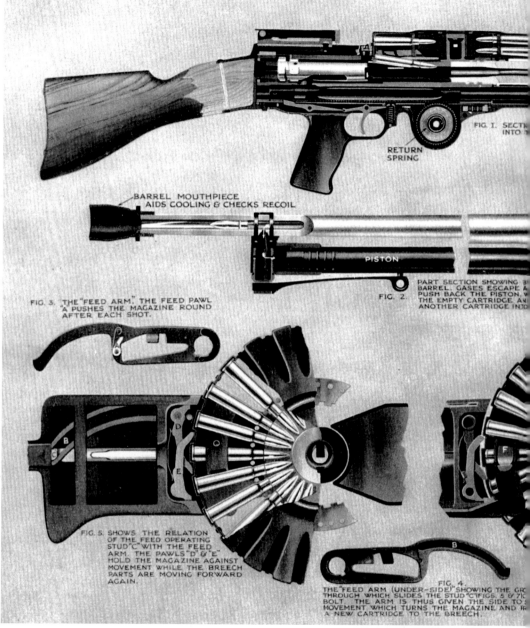

FIG. 1. SECTI[...]
INTO T[...]

RETURN
SPRING

BARREL MOUTHPIECE
AIDS COOLING & CHECKS RECOIL

PISTON

FIG. 2.

PART SECTION SHOWING B[...]
BARREL. GASES ESCAPE A[...]
PUSH BACK THE PISTON, W[...]
THE EMPTY CARTRIDGE AN[...]
ANOTHER CARTRIDGE INTO[...]

FIG. 3. THE "FEED ARM." THE FEED PAWL
"A" PUSHES THE MAGAZINE ROUND
AFTER EACH SHOT.

FIG. 5. SHOWS THE RELATION
OF THE FEED OPERATING
STUD "C" WITH THE FEED
ARM. THE PAWLS "D" & "E"
HOLD THE MAGAZINE AGAINST
MOVEMENT WHILE THE BREECH
PARTS ARE MOVING FORWARD
AGAIN.

FIG. 4.
THE "FEED ARM (UNDER-SIDE)" SHOWING THE GR[...]
THROUGH WHICH SLIDES THE STUD "C"(FIGS. 5 & 7)[...]
BOLT. THE ARM IS THUS GIVEN THE SIDE TO S[...]
MOVEMENT WHICH TURNS THE MAGAZINE AND F[...]
A NEW CARTRIDGE TO THE BREECH.

15. A sectional view of the Lewis gun. (*Taylor Library*)

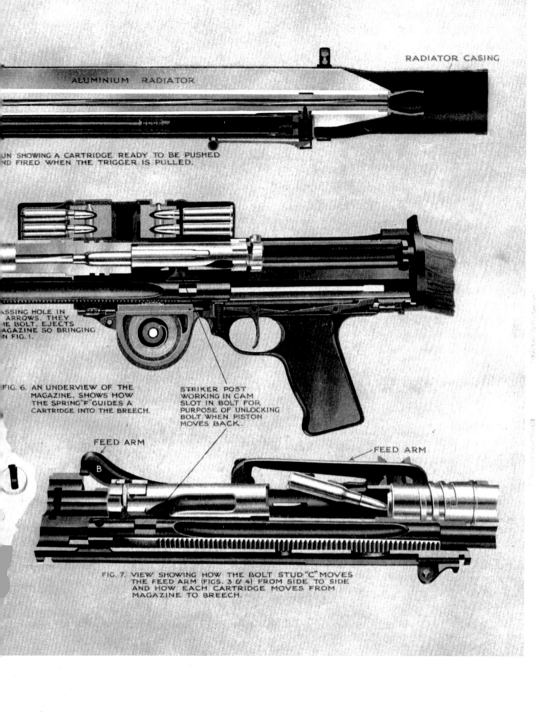

RADIATOR CASING

ALUMINIUM RADIATOR

...UN SHOWING A CARTRIDGE READY TO BE PUSHED
...ND FIRED WHEN THE TRIGGER IS PULLED.

...ASSING HOLE IN
...ARROWS. THEY
...HE BOLT, EJECTS
...AGAZINE SO BRINGING
...N FIG. 1.

FIG. 6. AN UNDERVIEW OF THE
MAGAZINE. SHOWS HOW
THE SPRING "F" GUIDES A
CARTRIDGE INTO THE BREECH.

STRIKER POST
WORKING IN CAM
SLOT IN BOLT FOR
PURPOSE OF UNLOCKING
BOLT WHEN PISTON
MOVES BACK.

FEED ARM

FEED ARM

FIG. 7. VIEW SHOWING HOW THE BOLT STUD "C" MOVES
THE FEED ARM (FIGS. 3 & 4) FROM SIDE TO SIDE
AND HOW EACH CARTRIDGE MOVES FROM
MAGAZINE TO BREECH.

16. A Lewis gun in the anti-aircraft role. It is being fired from a mount extemporized from a Vickers gun tripod and a cartwheel. The man on the right is using a Barr and Stroud range-finder, which was also used in conjunction with the Vickers gun. (*Taylor Library*)

17. A French CSRG gunner of the 53rd Colonial Infantry Regiment. The distinctive pouches on his belt each contain two magazines. He also carries a 7.65mm pistol purchased from Spain: standard issue for CSRG gunners. (*Photograph courtesy of the Imperial War Museum, London, Neg. no. Q 55032*)

8. An abandoned German machine gun nest. The MG08 is mounted on a simple trench-mount, of the type favoured for forward machine gun positions. The gun's former owners have disabled it by removing the feed block. (*Taylor Library*)

9. German prisoners. The man at the rear is shouldering an MG08/15 light machine gun. (*Taylor Library*)

20. German machine guns captured by the British. A captured Russian M1905 Maxim gun and a Madsen *Muskete*. (*Photograph courtesy of the Imperial War Museum, London, Neg. no. HU 93198*)

21. The Villar Perosa gun, here used as originally envisaged – with a heavy armoured shield. (*Photograph courtesy of the Imperial War Museum, London, Neg. no. Q 56999*)

22. The Austrian M12/P16 machine pistol, minus its detachable stock.

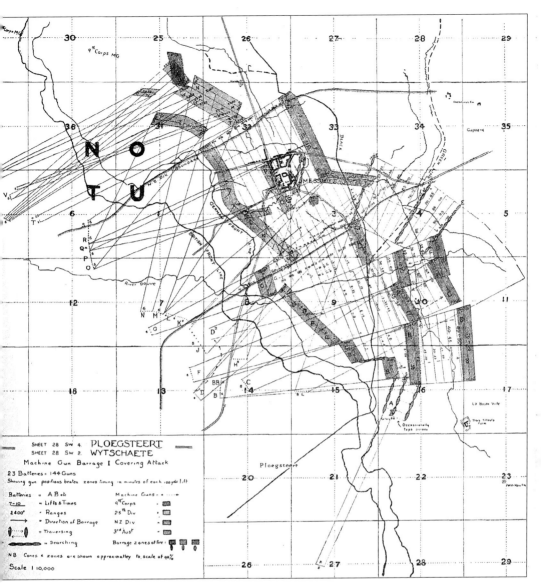

3. A diagram showing the machine gun scheme for II Anzac Corps at the Battle of Messines. The shaded areas were intended to receive standing barrages. The ladder-like successions of lines indicate creeping barrages.

24. Lieutenant Val Browning with his father's M1917 machine gun.

25. John M. Browning (left), the inventor of the M1918 automatic rifle, examines an early example of the weapon with Mr Burton, the Winchester expert on rifles. (*US Army Signal Corps Collection*)

26. General Odlum and other officers of 11th Canadian Brigade inspect a captured MP18 machine pistol. (*Photograph courtesy of the Imperial War Museum, London, Neg. no. CO 3035*)

7. An armoured 'Autocar' truck of the Canadian Motor Machine Gun Brigade going into action at the Battle of Amiens, 9 August 1918. (*Photograph courtesy of the Imperial War Museum, London, Neg. no. CO 3085*)

8. French and British troops with a Model 1914 Hotchkiss machine gun, during the retreat of 1918. The arrival of the enemy is evidently not imminent as the gun is not loaded and one of its crew is enjoying a pipe. (*Taylor Library*)

House-to-House Fighting in Fortified Pozières

When the tentacles of the German lines were crippled, the most costly and bitter fighting ensued in villages involved in the German system of defence. Such a place was Pozières, the whole village being turned into one great fort. House-to-house struggles were of frequent occurrence, and some of the Australian troops displayed again that glorious valour which won them fame in Gallipoli. This spirited drawing shows the capture of a German machine-gun in an improvised fort at Pozières.

29. The machine gun war as imagined by *The War Illustrated*, 1916. British troops burst into a strongpoint occupied by cowering German machine-gunners.

other light automatics did not. Nevertheless the tactic was on occasion used by the British and Germans. Both provided carrying slings for their light machine guns, and these were occasionally used to facilitate firing from the hip. The British pamphlet SS197 noted that, although the 'morale effect' of such fire was 'considerable', the 'material effect' was 'uncertain', and warned that it 'must be used with great discretion'. Notwithstanding these injunctions, occasional examples of successful use of 'walking fire' with the Lewis are recorded, particularly, it would appear, in the Canadian and ANZAC Corps.

The German response

The German Army was the last on the Western Front to be issued with an indigenously designed light automatic. In 1915 some Madsen guns had been acquired from neutral Denmark and were issued to two independent battalions, known as Musketen Bataillonen. These two battalions first saw service on in the Champagne region, and were later to see action during the Battle of the Somme. John Buchan, an early chronicler of that battle, makes a specific mention of their appearance on the Northern sector of the front on 1 July 1916: 'They had special light *Mousqueton* Battalions, armed only with machine-guns, who showed marvellous intrepidity, some even pushing their guns forward into no-man's-land to enfilade our advance.'[13] Overall, however, they do not appear to have proved successful – probably due to the fact that they were used as a defensive 'fire brigade' to seal off Allied break-ins, rather than in direct conjunction with counter-attacking infantry. The surviving Madsens were subsequently issued to mountain troops – but no more could be purchased from the Danes. Curiously, even as the Germans were taking the Madsen into service, the British Admiralty and War Office (the latter at the urging of Sir John French) were negotiating to build the Madsen under licence in Britain. In the event, nothing came of this plan.[14]

The main body of the German Army responded to the need for more portable forms of automatic firepower by adopting a range of 'trench mounts' (*hilfslaffeten*) for the MG08. These generally comprised a swivelling bracket mounted on a small wooden platform (or on metal feet), which was clamped to the water-jacket of the gun. These devices also permitted a wider range of traverse than the *schlitten*: a characteristic which was found useful for generating enfilade fire within the forward defensive zone. The French, prior to the appearance of the CSRG, had used bipods and monopods with their machine guns for the same purpose and at least one British unit is recorded as having extemporized trench mounts from ammunition boxes.[15] However, it was the Germans who made by far the most widespread use of such mounts. They were far from satisfactory. While they dispensed with the need to carry the heavy *schlitten* about, they prevented the machine gun from being used for anything other than short-range direct-fire. The appearance of the CSRG and, particularly, the Lewis, soon convinced the German High Command of the need to put a purpose-designed light machine gun into production. As one officer complained: 'The light British Lewis machine guns are superior to our heavy versions in mobility. Our machine gun is unfortunately too heavy to accompany our shock troops at their own pace.'[16] Another (after seeing the effectiveness of the Lewis on the Somme) opined that 'It is very desirable that our infantry should be equipped with a large number of light machine guns of this description.'[17]

Even as these pleas were made, the Army was on the verge of acting. In 1915 the Gewehr Prüfungs-Kommission had been instructed to select a suitable light automatic for issue to the German Army. For reasons of ease of manufacture and continuity of training, the committee's choice fell upon a lightened version of the existing Maxim design. This had been devised by team led by Friedrich von Merkatz, and was adopted for service as the MG08/15. The new gun utilized the same barrel and recoiling parts as its predecessor, but was lightened by reducing the diameter of the water-jacket (which now held three, rather than four, litres), altering the shape of the receiver and using thinner steel in its construction. The MG08/15 was fired from a bipod and was fitted with a wooden butt and a pistol grip. The decision to base the new weapon on an established design failed to bear immediate fruit, as production did not get fully under way until the end of 1916. Thereafter, however, output rose steeply, and 130,000 MG08/15s had been manufactured by the war's end; making it the most numerous German machine gun of the war.

The use of the proven Maxim system also ensured that the MG08/15 enjoyed superior reliability in combat conditions to either the Lewis or the CSRG. It could also offer a more sustained firepower, being water-cooled and fed from 100 round belts. The latter were held in a drum (*patronenkasten*) attached to the right of the gun, although standard 250 round MG08 belts were frequently used. The water was, however, not sufficient to permit the volume of sustained fire that a Vickers or MG08 could provide. The main drawback of the MG08/15 was that, as a German training pamphlet pointed out: 'its accuracy is strictly limited'.[18] A modern commentator (with much experience of shooting machine guns) states that 'it is extremely difficult to shoot the MG08/15 with any degree of accuracy'.[19] The reason for this is simple. The bipod of the weapon is attached at the rear, rather than the front, of the water-jacket. As a result, any unsteadiness on the part of the firer is magnified by the time its effects are transmitted to the muzzle of the gun; especially as the gun pivots at the point where the bipod touches the ground – 28cm below the line of the bore. A further failing of the MG08/15, its weight, was the inevitable result of the compromise solution that it represented. With its ammunition drum and bipod fitted, and its jacket filled, it weighed 22kg (compared with 14kg for a loaded Lewis and 10kg for the CSRG). With a normal complement of ammunition, tools and spares, the MG08/15 required a crew of four to serve it. These unfortunates were further burdened by the fact that they were ordered to carry rifles – so that their firepower would not be lost if the machine gun was put out of action. As General Ludendorff recalled: 'The infantry were supplied with a light machine-gun, which might well have been lighter and more simple, for it required too many men.'[20] In the last days of the war, an air-cooled version, the MG08/18, was issued in small quantities. Naturally this did much to solve the weight problem, but did not offer an equivalent potential for sustained fire.

In common with the British experience, the German Army found it necessary to take considerable pains to drive home the crucial differences between the machine gun and the light machine gun. It was stressed that 'By reason of its mechanical defects, the 08/15 light machine gun can never entirely take the place of the 08 machine gun.' Nevertheless it was 'indispensable' in mobile defence and could provide 'a valuable increase in the volume of fire' in the attack. In trench warfare it was firmly laid down that 'They should be posted in the front line, either in shell holes or in one of a number of alternative positions reconnoitred in advance.' Meanwhile, the MG08 was to be kept in concealed positions in the second and third lines of defence.[21]

Initially the issue of the new gun was limited to two guns per company – generally pooled in a single platoon. By the end of 1917, this number had, theoretically, risen to four – although British intelligence reports suggest that two or three was more normal, in the autumn at least. Only in 1918 were the benefits of volume production felt at the Front. By the spring of that year, units on the Western Front could hope to have as many as six MG08/15s per company – permitting each platoon to have two integral light machine guns. The vagaries of issue, wastage and breakdown naturally made such figures variable. For example, on 1 February 1918, the 60th Infantry Regiment had four guns per company on issue; this rose to five by the end of March and six shortly thereafter.[22]

The Bergmann gun

One significant variation existed to the use of Maxim designs within the German Army. This was the LMG15, manufactured by Theodor Bergmann

Waffenbau. This was a true light machine gun, with a loaded weight similar to that of the Lewis. It was air-cooled and operated on the short-recoil principle (employing a locking wedge mechanism, rather than the Maxim toggle). It size was kept compact by placing the trigger mechanism and pistol grip well forward, so that the rear of the receiver – to which a short wooden butt-piece was attached – lay along the firer's arm.

The LMG15 had been intended for use as an observer's gun in aircraft, but was found unsuitable for the role and, after around 1,500 had been produced, they were transferred to the infantry. In late 1916, 111 independent detachments were created to use them – each consisting of three sections of three guns. According to Allied intelligence reports, these were all sent to the Eastern Front – attached to newly raised divisions. The reasons for this deployment appear to be twofold. First, issue of the new MG08/15 was imminent, with the Western Front troops getting priority. Secondly there seems to have been a tendency to issue these air-cooled guns to troops serving where water-cooled weapons were more likely to freeze. This latter consideration is specifically mentioned in at least one German unit history.[23] For contrary reasons, the LMG15 was later issued to the Asien-Korps in Palestine, where water was likely to be scarce.

In 1917 an improved version of the LMG15, specifically intended for ground use, was introduced. The LMG15n.a. (*neuer art*) incorporated several improvements – the most notable of which were that it could now use the bipod and ammunition drum of the MG08/15. The original model had been fired from a rather spindly bipod attached to the barrel jacket, with the ammunition being fed from standard 250-round Maxim belts. Bergmann were not one of the five private concerns involved in the production of the MG08/15, so were permitted to continue manufacture of their light machine gun until the end of the war. It would appear that no more than 5,000 examples were in the field at any one time, although captured examples in Britain and Australia indicate that they eventually appeared on the Western Front – probably in the hands of units transferred from the East.[24]

Other captured weapons preserved in museum collections hint at further exotic exceptions to the dominance of the Maxim system within the German Army. These include Parabellum machine guns (more usually associated with use in aircraft), and even the odd Austrian Schwarzlose. Nevertheless, the quantities of such guns are trifling compared with the numbers of MG08/15s that saw issue. The ubiquity of the latter (and the sense that its failings prevented it from ever being loved by its users) is conveyed by fact that the expression *null-acht-fünfzehn* (0-8-15) passed into the German language; being used in much the same way as the modern British idiom 'bog-standard'.

The 08/15 also found its way into British military parlance. Although it was manufactured at two government arsenals and by five commercial contractors, by far the biggest producer was the Prussian state arsenal at Berlin-Spandau. As a consequence, the name 'Spandau' was the one most commonly found stamped on captured 08/15s, and became the generic English-language term for German light machine guns. This misnomer was carried into the Second World War – being applied to German guns manufactured long after the Spandau Gewehrfabrik had ceased manufacture of such weapons. The CSRG and Lewis gun achieved no such hold on posterity. The former was quietly replaced in 1924, being considered 'fundamentally deficient' and incapable of improvement. The Lewis survived longer – ultimately being replaced in front-line service by the Bren from 1937. Any resonance it now retains in British popular culture probably stems from its appearances in the 1970s comedy series 'Dad's Army'.

On the Eastern Front
The Western Front was the foundry in which the new concept of light automatic firepower was forged, but other armies soon became aware of its potential. The Austro-Hungarians followed the German lead by adapting their standard machine gun. The Schwarzlose was simply provided with a small tripod, or rudimentary bipod, and a shoulder stock. This weapon was known as the M7/12/16, and, like its German counterpart, utilized special 100-round belts. Additionally it could be fired from a pintle mounted on a wooden frame, which could also be used to transport the gun on the gunner's back. The arrival of this weapon in the field prompted a reorganization of infantry companies, wherein the fourth platoon of each company was converted into a pair of two-gun light machine gun sections. Each section (*Schwarm*) comprised a commander, a gunner, a gun carrier, two ammunition carriers, a water carrier and two riflemen. All members of the *Schwarm* were capable of firing the gun if necessary. Contemporary training instructions make clear that the K.u.K. Army had a good grasp of the discrete role of light machine guns. They were normally deployed by sections, with the two guns alternating their fire. The use of single guns was discouraged: conversely, the whole platoon fought together only in critical circumstances.[25]

In 1915 the Austro-Hungarian war ministry placed an order for 632 Madsen guns – probably with the intention of using them in mountain warfare against the Italians (who declared war on the Habsburg Empire on 23 May of that year). These were subsequently delivered, chambered for the Danish 6.5mm cartridge. In order to ensure continuity of ammunition supply it was decided to rechamber them. The 8mm Austrian service cartridge was deemed unsuitable,

as it was a rimmed cartridge. These are always more difficult to use in automatic weapons than rimless rounds – especially when they have to be fed from
box magazines. So the guns were instead converted to fire the German 7.92mm
rifle cartridge. This work delayed the issue of the guns, but they did eventually
see service with some alpine units.

The Russians were also in need of a light automatic – having only a few aged
Madsens at the outbreak of war. A plan to build the Madsen under licence did
not come to fruition. The Imperial Russian Army was, nevertheless, well aware
of the Lewis gun – having purchased some samples prior to August 1914. In
1917 the Russian Purchasing Commission in Britain placed orders for 10,000
.303-inch Lewis guns, and a further 1,200 in the Russian 7.62mm calibre. No
evidence survives of the actual number delivered before Russia descended into
revolution, although it is clear from surviving examples that not all were. The
Russians also attempted to purchase a 7.62mm version of the CSRG. However,
the potential difficulty of rechambering the weapon resulted in them accepting
it in the French 8mm calibre – of which 3,802 were delivered. Obviously these
numbers were a drop in the ocean as far as the actual requirements of the
Russian Army went. Their impact was further circumscribed by a lack of
spares and the difficulties of ammunition supply. Certainly this rather pitiful
assortment of weapons was in no way able to effect any significant change in the
organization of the Russian infantry.

This sorry picture is nevertheless enlivened by one very notable development in firearms technology. In the pre-war era a Russian designer, V G
Fedorov, had been attempting to develop a self-loading rifle. He realized that
the standard Russian 7.62mm cartridge was too powerful for his needs.
Furthermore it had a potentially awkward rimmed case. Consequently Fedorov
developed a rifle that chambered a rimless 6.5mm cartridge of his own
devising. This rifle was never developed beyond the experimental stage, but
Russia's desperate need for automatic firepower during the war gave Fedorov's
concept renewed relevance. In an attempt to fill the gap between the bolt-action
rifle and the Maxim gun, he redesigned his rifle as a selective-fire weapon, and
chambered it for the Japanese 6.5mm cartridge. This ammunition was in
plentiful supply, as Russia had purchased large quantities of Japanese rifles to
make up for the shortfall in her own production.

The Fedorov automatic rifle was a recoil-operated weapon, in which two
'locking-plates', which secured the bolt to the barrel as the gun was fired, were
tipped by the rearward movement of the barrel to unlock the action. The
Fedorov employed a 25-round box magazine, and was fitted with a wooden
stock featuring a vertical fore-grip.[26] From December 1916 the Fedorov automatic rifle (along with some of his self-loaders) underwent field trials in the

hands of the 189th Infantry Regiment. Orders for the production of large quantities of the automatic rifle were subsequently given, but the Revolution intervened. In January 1918 the Bolshevik Chief Artillery Directorate sent Fedorov to organize production of his gun in the town of Kovrov – ironically in facilities which had been intended for the licensed-manufacture of Madsen LMGs. Production was painfully slow and, although the Fedorov saw some use by Bolshevik forces in the Russian Civil War, only 3,200 examples had been built by the time manufacture ceased in 1925.[27]

The real significance of the Fedorov automatic rifle is that it presaged an entirely new form of infantry weapon: the assault rifle. Indeed, the Fedorov had the essential characteristics of modern assault rifles – it offered either semi or fully automatic fire, and it was chambered for a cartridge of less than full power. The term 'assault rifle' appears to have been coined by none other than Adolf Hitler, when he renamed the German MP44 the *Sturmgewehr* 44. The Russians have always known them by the name *Avtomat* – a term that was first used during the 1920s to describe the Fedorov rifle.

American controversy

On the other side of the world, matters were, if anything, still more confused. The US Army did of course already have a light machine gun in service: namely the Benét-Mercié, or US Automatic Machine Rifle, Model of 1909. Attempts to get the indigenous Lewis gun considered for US service had foundered on the existence of this gun and a history of personal animosity between Colonel Lewis and the chief of the US Ordnance Department: General William Crozier. The failure to interest the US Army or Navy in his gun had been the reason behind Lewis and his backers' decision to enter the European arms market.

In early 1916, the Benét-Mercié and, by extension, the Ordnance Department, suffered something of a public relations disaster. In the early hours of the morning of 9 March, the small border-town of Columbus in New Mexico was attacked and burnt by Mexican *Villista* insurgents, under General Ramon Banda Quesada. The town was defended by elements of the US 13th Cavalry Regiment – including its machine gun platoon, with four 'machine rifles'. Although the attackers were driven off with no little loss, the defenders experienced problems in keeping all their guns in action. A subsequent official report indicated that the machine rifles had frequently jammed due to the difficulty of feeding them with their strips of ammunition in the dark. The press had a field day with this information – caustically referring to the Benét-Mercié as the 'Daylight Gun'.

For the remainder of the year, a public controversy raged, stoked by both Crozier and Lewis (the latter abetted by General Leonard Wood – a Lewis gun advocate). This involved, in the words of the *New York Times* 'considerable muck-raking and not a little propaganda'. Effectively, there was probably little to choose between the two guns in terms of combat-worthiness. While the Army stuck with the Benét-Mercié, the Navy did begin to purchase Lewis guns for issue to the Marine Corps at the start of 1917. These were manufactured by the Savage Arms Company, which was already producing the Lewis under licence, for sale to Canada.

The United States Army was ill-prepared for the war which it entered on 6 April 1917. None of the current inventory of automatic firearms available were considered fit for service overseas. As a consequence, the first twelve US divisions to sail for France had to be equipped, on arrival, with Hotchkiss machine guns and CSRG machine rifles. Each US infantry platoon was now provided with an 'Automatic Rifle Section' with four CSRG teams, organized in two squads. The 8mm CSRG proved as useful to the Americans as it had to their allies, and it was decided to produce a version chambered for the US .30-inch cartridge. Gladiator manufactured 18,000 of these (known as the Model 1918) between January and May 1918. Unfortunately the .30 CSRG turned out to be something of a disaster, being highly liable to jam when fired in bursts. The reason for this was a failure to extract spent cartridge cases – generally shearing off the cartridge head and leaving its body stuck fast in the chamber. Modern research has confirmed that, extraordinarily, errors were made in the dimensioning of the chamber during the reworking of the gun to the new calibre.[28] The resulting inexact fit was naturally exacerbated as the barrel began to expand when heated by firing. It would appear that the problem became sufficiently widely known for the Americans to place their reliance upon the 16,000 8mm Chauchats already in their hands, rather than in the new guns. It could probably be argued that the US experience of the .30 CSRG was a major factor in forming the subsequent bad reputation of the weapon as a whole – particularly given the American domination of the field of firearms writing during the later part of the twentieth century.

In an attempt to defuse the simmering Crozier–Lewis controversy, the US War Department created a Machine Gun Board, to make recommendations as to which automatic weapons were most suitable for issue to the US Army. This board carried out comparative trials in May 1917. In their report they invited 'special attention to the tactical possibilities of the Colt's automatic machine rifle'. This weapon had been designed by none other than John M Browning, and has entered history as the Browning Automatic Rifle (BAR). The BAR was a gas-operated weapon, in which the bolt was locked by a locking arm. This arm was attached by a hinged link to a slide that was operated by the gas piston. As the gas pressure drove the slide to the rear, the link pulled the locking arm out of engagement with a 'shoulder' in the roof of the receiver to unlock the breech. A twenty-round box magazine was used.

The BAR weighed just under 9kg loaded – heavy for a shoulder-fired weapon, but light in comparison with other 'machine-rifles' of the day. It was also robust and reliable in comparison with the Lewis and the CSRG; its magazine was also superior. Both Browning and the army had visions of achieving a widespread issue of the BAR, with groups of automatic-riflemen advancing across no man's land while suppressing the defender's fire with 'walking fire'. A special automatic rifleman's belt was introduced for use with both the BAR and the CSRG – featuring a metal 'cup' for supporting the butt when firing from the hip. Sadly for the infantrymen of the AEF, the BAR was withheld from issue in the field until the autumn of 1918.

Two reasons (not necessarily mutually exclusive) have been offered for this. Most likely it was simply the case that it was intended to re-equip and retrain the AEF as a whole, when sufficient stock of the new weapon had been assembled. It was, after all, generally expected that the war would continue into 1919. Claims have also been made that Pershing himself insisted on holding back issue of the BAR, for fear that it would fall into enemy hands and inspire them to build a copy. If so, he can perhaps be forgiven for not realizing that such a thing would have been beyond the capacity of the German war industry in 1918. Furthermore, the BAR had certainly been developed in a climate of secrecy, with ratification of its patents suspended until the war's end. Whatever the case, the first use of the Browning automatic rifle took place only during the Meuse-Argonne offensive of September 1918. At the time of the Armistice the 8mm CSRG remained the most widely issued machine rifle in AEF.

The birth of the submachine-gun

Portable automatic firepower was not only of concern to the armies engaged on the Western and Eastern Fronts. Indeed, south of the Alps, a remarkable development had taken place as early as 1914. On 8 April of that year, the designer Revelli had patented an entirely new type of weapon. This was a fully automatic gun, operating on the blowback principle, and chambered for pistol ammunition. These characteristics give it a claim to having been the first submachine-gun[29] ever devised. However the Villar Perosa (as Revelli's gun has become known, from its first producer) differed from modern submachine-guns in several ways. First it was constructed as a twin – with two guns bracketed together, linked by a single trigger unit. Secondly, it was not shoulder (or hip) fired, but was equipped with machine-gun-like grips and a double-thumb trigger. Furthermore it was originally issued with a 26kg armoured shield!

Nevertheless, the Villar Perosa's system of operation, and its use of pistol ammunition fed from box magazines, indisputably prefigure the weapon-type known today as the submachine-gun. Revelli employed a 'delayed-blowback' system in the gun, wherein the bolt is obliged to overcome a mechanical disadvantage before opening. This was effected in the Villar Perosa by a lug on the bolt, which rode in a track cut in the receiver, and which twisted through 45 degrees as the bolt-head met the chamber. In fact the effect of this arrangement proved negligible, and the weapon was notable for its extremely high rate of fire. The distinctive sound it made resulted in it being nicknamed the *Pernacchia* – the Italian expression for 'blowing a raspberry'. The magazines used contained 25 rounds but, at a cyclic-rate of over 1,200 rounds per minute, it required a man of unusual dexterity and self-control to avoid firing the whole lot off with a single press of the trigger.

Despite the Villar Perosa's idiosyncrasies it was taken into service by the Italian Army – who could see the advantage of a light automatic weapon in the war which, from May 1915, they were to fight in the Alps, the Dolomites and the rugged terrain of the Isonzo Valley. Production was slow at first, and the 350 guns that appeared in 1915 were sent for use in aircraft, due to a delay in the manufacture of their armoured shields. As this fact would suggest, the proposed employment of the Villar Perosa in the field was anything but submachine-gun-like in its nature. Instead it was expected to provide defensive firepower in positional warfare. Sadly this was something that it was ill equipped to do – due to its inability to conduct sustained fire and the weakness of its ammunition. Pistol ammunition is only effective at relatively short ranges and the Italian 9mm Glisenti cartridge was not noted for its power. Hence the Villar Perosa did not create an immediate impact when issue to the infantry commenced in April 1916.

Its users soon learnt, however, to maximize the new weapon's potential for portability and mobility. The heavy shield was swiftly discarded and, from June 1916, a bipod was adopted. By the close of 1916, 946 units were in service. In 1917 further impetus was given to the development of suitable tactics for the Villar Perosa by the creation of the Reparti d'Assalto – the Arditi – a force of elite assault troops. The Arditi seized upon the Villar Perosa as a potential provider of firepower in the assault. To facilitate this, alternative mounts were developed for the weapon: first, a sort of tray which supported the gun in front of the firer while advancing; secondly an improved, flexible, bipod. Eventually a wooden stock with a rifle-style butt was fitted to some examples. Around 15,000 Villar Perosa guns were produced in total.[30] Following the disastrous defeat at Caporetto in November 1917, the Italians also acquired 2,000 Lewis guns from Britain, and created fifty specialist companies to employ them. The Italians also purchased significant quantities of the French CSRG.

The shortcomings of the Villar Perosa led the Italian Army to request the Beretta arms company to look into the possibility of improving on the concept. The task was deputed to a young designer, Tullio Marengoni. He took a single Villar Perosa barrel and action and coupled it with a conventional wooden stock and trigger mechanism to create the Beretta Moschetto M1918. This came in two forms – a semi-automatic carbine and a submachine-gun; the latter boasting two triggers, one for automatic fire and a second for single shots. The weapon was issued during 1918, but the quantity that saw service remains obscure.

A machine pistol

The Austro-Hungarian Army too, swiftly became aware of the potential benefits of man-portable automatic firepower in mountainous terrain. According to at least one account, a Major Fuchs, commander of the 2nd Innsbruck Standschützenbataillon (Tyrolean militia), was so convinced of this that he took it upon himself to provide a source.[31] He was aware that a version of the Steyr M12 service pistol with an extended, 16-round, magazine capacity had been issued to the army air service. He somehow acquired eight of these weapons, which he issued to an assault platoon of his battalion. They proved successful and, circumventing official channels, he wrote directly to the Steyr factory, requesting a version of this gun capable of firing fully automatically. His request bore fruit in the form of the Repetierpistole M12/P16. This weapon featured a selector lever, permitting it to fire fully automatically, or as a self-loader. A detachable shoulder-stock-cum-holster was provided. The first issue of these weapons (to Fuchs's own unit) took place in February 1916. By the end of the war 9,873 M12/P16 pistols had been issued on the Tyrolean and Isonzo Fronts.

This figure might have been higher, had the War Ministry not begun to interest itself in machine pistols – despite apparent official disapproval of any move away from aimed fire.[32] Certainly there are few weapons less easy to hold on aim than fully automatic handguns, the muzzles of which exhibit an uncontrollable urge to rise as a burst of fire is discharged. This fact notwithstanding, official tests were carried out with the M12/P16 and other patterns of machine pistol based on the Hungarian Frommer pistol. This had the effect of holding back production of the former. Meanwhile, attempts were being made to develop a copy of the Villar Perosa. The Austro-Hungarian Army – particularly its assault units – was already pressing captured examples of the Italian weapon into service. The Austrian copy, known as the Sturmpistole M18, was distributed among light machine gun platoons in 1918, but appears to have arrived too late to see any meaningful active service.

Chapter 5

'Like the Whistle of a Great Wind'

You must fight your guns in Batteries from a Grand Divisional Pool
Give them fifty bob protractors too, made at the Small Arms School
With these and other blessings of a Centralised Control
We'll drive the Hun across the Rhine and leave him up the pole
                        (From a 'Machine Gun Corps Song' preserved
                            in the Lindsay Papers at the Tank Museum)

The year 1917 witnessed the maturation of the tactical advances made by all sides as lessons learnt during the battles of the previous two years were absorbed. The British and French entered the year full of hope that they now had sufficient materiel (particularly artillery and shells) and the correct tactical 'recipe' to achieve a breakthrough on the Western Front. As it turned out however, German defensive tactics had developed too. By the end of the Somme battles, the German command had no longer insisted upon potentially costly, immediate local counter-attacks. By 1917, whole divisions were kept in readiness to launch large-scale counter-attacks at the apposite moment. The success or failure of this policy depended on the correct positioning of these reserves – beyond the threat of destruction by artillery fire, but near enough to be launched into the assault before the enemy had consolidated his gains. In a further response to the lessons of the Somme, changes were made in the employment of machine guns. The tendency to position them at the rear of the defensive zone was confirmed. Furthermore, they were distributed 'chequer-wise' rather than being grouped in redoubts as they had been on the Somme. Their function was not to be a rock on which attacks could founder, but to provide fire support for the counter-attacking units. In March 1917 this system received a further tweak, when (reminding us of the primacy of artillery on the battlefield) it was ordered that the Maschinengewehr-Scharfschützen detachments be used to 'protect the artillery'. This placed them firmly at the rear of the defensive area – typically between 1,500 and 2,000 metres from the front line. Here they could not only screen the artillery positions, but offer a rallying point for any troops driven out of their positions, and the basis of fire support for subsequent counter-attacks.

The French spring offensive on the Chemin des Dames was aborted after it encountered this new system – having failed miserably to live up to the expectations engendered by its author, General Nivelle. The commander of the French II Colonial Corps found his troops 'fixed in place' by the 'deadly fire of numerous machine guns' located in the reverse-slope positions: 'Any attempts to regain forward movement fail as they arrive on the line covered by the enemy machine guns.'[1] An additional and novel threat faced by the French in this offensive was the large-scale use by the Germans of the MG08/15 light machine gun to stiffen their forward defensive zone. This new addition to the German armoury was to prove of more than merely defensive utility, however, as its mobility greatly enhanced the firepower of the German infantry in the counter-attack.

To the north, the complementary offensive launched at Arras by the British and Dominion armies had more mixed results. Remarkable advances were achieved on the first day of the battle, due to meticulously planned barrages and the incorrect positioning of the German reserves. However, the break-in could not be converted into a breakthrough. The Germans soon mustered their counter-attacking forces, and the British found it difficult to push the artillery forward to support any further advances. This set of circumstances was to be repeated, with variations, throughout 1917. One lesson learnt was that, despite the fact that the holy grail of 'breakthrough' remained unattainable, offensive firepower had now developed to such an extent that defenders were effectively powerless to do any more than delay the break-in of attackers into their positions. The upshot of this was that most Allied successes of 1917 were the product of 'bite and hold' operations, with limited objectives. Machine guns were to play an important role in these 'set-piece' battles. As the British Official History notes: 'Machine gun barrages fired over the heads of the advancing infantry had now become universal in offensive operations.'

The set-pieces
The capture of the commanding heights of Vimy Ridge, between 9 and 12 April 1917, is one of the most enduring epics of the Western Front; particularly as it has become inextricably linked with the birth of Canadian nationhood. Not so well known is the part played in the operation by machine guns, firing what one British officer described as 'probably the first really great barrage'. Although British troops played a significant part in the success at Vimy, this barrage was truly Canadian in origin. Its orchestrator was of course Raymond Brutinel. Since the previous October, this pioneering machine-gunner had held the position of Corps Machine Gun Officer to the Canadian Corps. Due

to a combination of the force of his personality and the support of his corps commander, Lieutenant-General Julian Byng, Brutinel wielded considerably more influence than was enjoyed at the time by his British counterparts – who faced a struggle to organize large-scale schemes of machine gun fire. For the Vimy operation Brutinel had at his disposal 294 guns of the Canadian Corps and a further sixty-four from the British 5th Division. Of these, 104 were to accompany the attacking troops, and twenty-four would be held in reserve. The remaining 230 guns were to fire barrages. For command and control purposes, these were split into units of no more than eight guns each. A creeping barrage, coordinated with the artillery barrage, was to be fired during the assault. Additionally 'Protective' (or SOS) barrages were planned to fall ahead of sequence of objective 'lines'. The later of these, including the Final Protective Barrage, were too far in advance of the assembly area for the gunners to emplace themselves prior to the assault. As a consequence, the batteries firing them were obliged to advance to preselected positions once the attack had begun to make headway.

The creeping barrage was timed to catch the German defenders as they emerged from their dugouts once the heavy artillery barrage had passed over them. The pre-war British machine gun theorist R V K Applin (by this time a lieutenant-colonel in the Machine Gun Corps) later described the effect of this barrage to an American audience:

> trench after trench, back trenches, switch trenches, communicating trenches, were found full of dead Germans, and those dead Germans were found with rifle bullets in the breast, nothing down by their feet, always in the breast, showing that they were breast-high over their entrenchments when hit. Now, not a single rifle was fired by our men in the attack; they go over the top in silence with the bayonet; so that that was all done by machine-gun fire.[2]

Applin had visited the scene himself, shortly after the battle, and had spoken to Brutinel, who stressed the importance of his SOS fire scheme. He also talked to officers who had benefited from the support of this fire: 'they were all talking of absolutely nothing but this machine-gun barrage, and how the Huns melted away before it'. Thus the inevitable German counter-attacks failed to dislodge the Canadians from their newly won positions. Nevertheless the Germans' own defensive machine gun fire had proved effective once again. Bill Rawling has pointed out that it caused the majority of Canadian casualties – despite suspected machine gun emplacements being targeted by single 'spare' 18-pounder field guns; which had been assigned specifically to this task.

The Australians were not slow in appreciating the usefulness of big machine gun barrages. At Bullecourt in May 1917, the 2nd Australian Division, by borrowing guns from the 5th Australian Division, managed to assemble no less than ninety-six guns to support an attack by two of its brigades. Eighty-four of these were used to provide a supporting barrage.

The grandest set-piece barrage of all, however, was not to occur until the following month. It took place during the Second Army's successful assault on Messines Ridge on 7 June 1917. It was for this operation that Second Army workshops produced depression-stops for mounting on the crossheads of guns nominated for barrage fire. These prevented the gun from being accidentally depressed below a level set to ensure the safety of intervening troops and, according to a report from 19th Division, they 'greatly increased the confidence of all ranks'.

Properly speaking, it was three barrages in one, as each of the corps involved in the attack (IX Corps, X Corps and II Anzac Corps) planned its own machine gun support. The combined total of guns in action was 454 (out of the 700 available to the three corps), and it was estimated that a staggering 15 million rounds of ammunition would be required. The three corps devised their own barrage plans according to the terrain and objectives with which they were faced. In the north X Corps fired four standing barrages, each 500 yards ahead of their four successive objective lines. IX Corps, in the centre, fired a standing barrage on the ridge itself, and a creeping barrage to accompany their advance.

The most refined plan was devised by none other than Colonel Applin, who was machine gun officer of II Anzac Corps, tasked with the seizure of the village of Messines itself. A standing barrage was established to protect the southern flank of the attack, an enfilade barrage was brought to bear on the rear approaches to the village and, finally, a creeping barrage was fired to harrow the German lines 400 yards ahead of the artillery creeping barrage. Two of the three barrage groups advanced onto the ridge itself once it was captured, to provide support for the second phase of the operation.

When the machine gun barrages struck home, their potency seems to have surprised even the machine-gunners themselves. IX Corps zealously recorded the effects of its barrage for future reference. One officer from 16th Division asserted that 'I have made a careful examination of certain portions of the ground where the barrage was playing and found dead men and horses, telegraph poles and trees riddled with bullets.'[3] The officer commanding 33rd MG Company (11th Division) noted that 'large numbers of dead were found to have been killed by our MG fire, while apparently attempting to go back from their trenches'. At II Anzac Corps, doubtless bearing in mind the injunctions of Brutinel, Applin ensured that his SOS barrages were well prepared. These were brought to bear on German counter-attacks after the ridge was taken. Applin later described their effect in dramatic terms:

> an artillery observer in the front-line trench told me – that on the S.O.S. going up, the machine gun barrage came down instantly, while the rocket was still up in the air, exactly like a heavy shower of hail, and he said it was the most curious sight he had ever seen. This barrage came down, the weather was dry, and the dust flew, and the masses of Germans, he said, seemed to eddy and then melt away, and there was nothing left.[4]

Colonel Luxford bore similar witness the outcome of the barrage fired against the main German counter-attack, on the evening of 7 June; which he regarded as 'phenomenal'. He concluded that:

> Although the [machine] gunners cannot claim to the whole honour of smashing the counter-attack so completely that it withered away before it reached our advanced lines, they can nevertheless say that their fire played a large part in producing this wonderful success.[5]

Universal tactical developments

Barrage fire on the scale of Vimy and Messines could not but attract attention to itself. A demonstration barrage was fired on the dunes at Camiers at the request of Sir Douglas Haig who, furthermore, insisted that all his Corps commanders should attend. French observers were treated to a similar demonstration, with the result that the technique was introduced into the French Army with admirable dispatch. As early as 26 April 1917 the Headquarters of the French Armies of the North and North East issued a note recommending the adoption of the tactic at the highest level: 'The High Command must take the question into its hands, orient the ideas, and develop the education of the machine gun officers in the practice of this kind of fire.'[6] They even went so far as to suggest that barrage fire 'allows a very considerable economy of artillery ammunition, and its effect is at least as certain and more demoralizing by its continuity than that of cannon'. An astonishing admission for the army that had gone to war wedded to the belief that its field guns were the supreme arbiter of battle! The French subsequently created their own machine gun school near Camiers, where barrage fire techniques were taught. Barrages were used with notable success by the French in their offensive operations on the north bank of the Meuse at Verdun during August 1917. Further evidence of the spread of indirect fire techniques within the French Army is offered by the fact that barrage fire was later employed by the divisions of the American

Expeditionary Force that were equipped with Hotchkiss Machine guns and trained by French instructors.

Naturally the Germans were alive to the threat posed by the growing sophistication of Allied offensive tactics. During the autumn of 1917 two machine guns were issued to each artillery battery for close defence purposes, in case Allied attacks penetrated as far as their positions (as had famously occurred at 'Battery Valley' during the Battle of Arras – resulting in the loss of more than thirty guns). The British were to make a similar issue of Lewis guns to their artillery units in early 1918. This move proved a success and some officers (such as General Horne of First Army) advocated the issue of Lewis guns to Royal Engineer Field Companies and other non-infantry formations who might find themselves in contact with the enemy.[7] Meanwhile, the firepower of the German infantry was, as ever, developed primarily from machine guns. Contemporary German estimates of the consumption of ammunition by machine guns as opposed to rifles ranged from two-thirds to an amazing nine-tenths.[8] Even during the course of successful attacks Allied infantrymen could expect to suffer from the attentions of the German machine-gunners. Indeed, the most complete victory of all – the seizure of Messines Ridge – was marred by casualties inflicted upon the victors by long-range machine gun fire, as they crowded onto the newly won heights. Interestingly, as events on the Somme had presaged, German defensive tactics were frequently more reliant upon short-range machine gun fire. In a calculated exchange of long fields of fire for concealment and the potential for surprise, their positions were frequently on reverse slopes (the choice of forward or reverse slope position was actually predicated by the needs of artillery observers[9]). Light machine guns – typically firing from shell holes – would provide some initial resistance in forward areas; but the bulk of the defensive fire would emanate from emplacements in the battle zone, to the rear of the forward defensive zone. These were constructed with the hope of avoiding prior observation and offered all-round fields of fire, so that attacking troops could be caught in enfilade. As one German tactician noted: 'The unexpected opening of fire of a single machinegun under the efficient leadership, even if served by only a few cool men, has several times been the decisive factor in victory and defeat.'

However, in tandem with this policy, by late 1917 the Germans were evidently beginning to make use of barrage and indirect fire. Some units had already been experimenting with indirect fire on an *ad hoc* basis.[10] However, it was not until the Third Battle of Ypres that such tactics came to be mentioned in a British intelligence report. This suggested that 'There is evidence that the enemy is beginning to copy our methods of indirect fire.' Prisoners captured in the latter part of that battle asserted that selected machine-gunners were being sent on courses to be instructed in these techniques. At the same time a graph giving clearances for overhead fire was captured. Early in the following year, further evidence was found in German written orders. An order from the HQ of German XIII Corps in April 1917 instructed that 'The emplacements of the heavy machine guns must be sited so that the machine guns can, in the first place, support the assaulting infantry by means of overhead fire.' By 20 May Ludendorff himself was endorsing the use of indirect fire, asserting that 'it can be used with advantage in the preparation for and even in the first phase of the attack itself'.[11] The British Official History records that the German 16th Division used its attached Maschinengewehr-Scharfschützen Abteilung to fire an effective overhead barrage against attacking troops of XVIII Corps near Poelcappelle on 9 October 1917. In 1918 the Germans began to issue a sophisticated set of purpose-made indirect-fire equipment to their machine-gunners. This consisted of a dial sight (for mounting on the optical sight bracket of the gun), a compass-like fire director (for mounting on the sledge-mount) and a rather intimidating protractor. These were to be used in conjunction with a traverse-limitation bracket, which had to be fixed to the receiver of the gun.[12] The history of the Saxon 104th Infantry Regiment states that this equipment became available from March 1918 onwards.[13] Compared with the somewhat extemporized nature of the indirect fire equipment employed by the MGC, the appearance of these devices indicates a very serious commitment to the principle of indirect machine-gunnery on the part of the German Army.

Thus Captain Dunn's fears that the Germans might copy the British MG barrage were being realized, even as he was confiding them to his diary. Fortunately for the Allies, their exploitation of the technique had begun too late to make a major impact. Nevertheless these developments might be considered as the most resounding endorsement of the value of British barrage fire techniques – all the more so as the Germans continued to pursue their interest in the tactic after the war. Indirect fire subsequently formed an important element of the tactics recommended for the new generation of German machine guns that saw service during the Second World War.[14] This would hardly have been the case if Allied barrage fire had been as ineffective as some of its detractors claimed.

The machine-gunners of all sides were obliged to be aware of the threats posed by new military technologies which, although in their infancy during the first two years of the war, had now become more fully developed. From the latter part of 1916 the need for anti-aircraft defence became apparent, and all armies began to assign machine guns to this purpose. Some lighter automatics were also found to be effective in this role. For instance, each British infantry battalion headquarters was now provided with four Lewis guns for AA defence.

As the war progressed, machine-gunners themselves became increasingly the target of ground-attack aircraft. The seriousness of this threat becomes apparent in tactical instructions. Machine gun officers were exhorted to take more care in the positioning of their emplacements. For example, standing crops – which had formerly been seen as a suitable hiding place for a machine gun – were now to be avoided, as such positions were so readily spotted from the air. A further technological innovation was the tank – which had, of course, been invented specifically to neutralize the machine gun threat. It was the Germans who were on the receiving end of this new engine of destruction and, as a consequence, they began to issue armour-piercing ammunition. Tactical instructions specifically laid down the quantities of these S.m.K. (*Sptizgeschoss mit Stahlkern*) cartridges that needed to be kept available in each machine gun post. Indeed, in the frequent absence of more specialized anti-tank weaponry, German machine guns might well have had claim to being the principal tank 'killers' of the Great War. Finally, in 1917, chemical warfare plumbed new depths of unpleasantness with the introduction of mustard gas. The persistent nature of this agent necessitated the careful stripping and cleaning (generally with chloride of lime) of any firearms exposed to it and it could, of course, also contaminate machine gun belts and other accessories.

Third Ypres

The Third Battle of Ypres, or the Battle of Passchendaele as it has become commonly known, looms second only to the Somme in the popular perception of the Great War – as an 'epic of mud' in which men were pushed to the limits of human endurance in pursuit of an illusory decision. It is not often appreciated that, despite the terrible weather that dogged the beginning and end of the battle, this operation was conducted on a far more sophisticated tactical basis than the Somme and Verdun battles of the previous year. Once again, this more advanced form of warfare was both reflected in and exemplified by the use of machine guns.

The Ypres salient did not witness the use of large-scale set-piece machine gun barrages covering the whole frontage of attacks. Instead, machine gun schemes became primarily a divisional affair and were targeted at specific objectives. Provision was also made to 'switch' the fire of batteries of guns onto areas where attacks had become stalled, or where flanks were exposed – even where these danger-spots lay within the area of neighbouring divisions. In the light of the successes at Vimy and Messines, cooperation with the artillery was encouraged. In fact, during certain phases of the Ypres offensive, the machine guns of both sides gained enhanced significance, as the artillery began to circumscribe its own effectiveness, first, by churning the battlefield into a morass in which it was hugely difficult to move guns or fire effectively (platforms had to be built for individual artillery pieces), and secondly, by repeatedly destroying the telephone lines through which its fire was controlled. Machine guns therefore, being both more mobile and, usually, in closer contact with the infantry than was the artillery, took on added importance.

Nevertheless, an unprecedented concentration of artillery was packed into the relatively limited confines of the Ypres battlefield, and machine-gunners could not operate beyond its reach. The British pamphlet SS201, which summarized elements of the battle specific to machine guns, noted the vulnerability to artillery bombardment of batteries of guns set up for barrage fire. Arthur Russell personally experienced this during the offensive, recalling that a 'battery of four guns firing the machine-gun barrage was spotted by the German artillery observers and the vicinity of the gun positions was boxed in by a heavy and concentrated storm of shell fire. All the four machine guns were destroyed, six gunners killed, four terribly wounded and several received cushy blighties.'[15] One response to this threat was for machine gun batteries to fire shorter but more intense barrages, thus limiting the amount of time for which the machine-gunners were exposed to artillery observation. The weather conditions also impinged heavily upon the activities of machine-gunners. The principal reason for this was the need to move large quantities of ammunition up to the gun positions. Each case of 1,000 .303-inch cartridges weighed over 38kg. As one neared the front line at Ypres, limbers and even mules became useless, and manpower became the only option. As previously mentioned, special shelters had to be built to ensure that ammunition belts were kept dry while being filled. Not surprisingly the fragile Lewis gun suffered from the muddy conditions more than the more robust Maxim-system guns used by the MGC and the Germans. This is emphasized in a report from the Officer Commanding 58th Division listing the reasons for a failed attack: 'C) Oblique hostile machine-gun fire was very effective. D) The only Lewis gun succeeded in getting into action was useless in three minutes. E) All uncovered rifles were useless, all covered rifles ditto within ten minutes.'[16]

The intense nature of the 'Fourth Battle of Flanders', as the Germans called it, is exemplified by the Battle of Polygon Wood, which took place between 25 and 27 September 1917. An important eyewitness account is given by Colonel Hutchinson. He vividly described the gruelling task of bringing up 700,000 rounds of ammunition: 'under sudden and violent shell-storms, or subject to the annoyance of being sniped by field guns, my machine gunners man-handled the boxes across a mile of shell-pocked land to the positions. The burden was most severe, following, as it did, a march from bivouacs over the broken pitted, mud-covered track of eight miles.' Hutchinson was commanding the machine guns of 33rd Division, but was, initially, to fire in support of operations by 23rd Division. His men suffered heavily from enemy artillery fire while conducting this barrage. On 25 September the German 50th Reserve Division launched a pre-emptive attack on the British lines – at the precise moment that the 33rd Division was relieving the 23rd. Just before dawn, following an artillery barrage, the Germans attacked with, according to Hutchinson, 'outstanding gallantry'. They advanced straight into the direct fire of the independent 207th Machine Gun Company, which had been placed under Hutchinson's command. According to his account 'the enemy was so far committed to the assault that he could not retire, but must advance. Low flying aeroplanes, however, soon detected the battery and both by machine gun action and directing artillery fire upon the gunners the enemy inflicted severe casualties among them.' The German attack was eventually held, and the next day the 33rd Division machine-gunners fired an 'elaborate' barrage, which involved moving forty-eight guns forward 800 yards to new positions – by no means an inconsiderable task in the salient. Subsequent SOS barrages were notably successful, and repulsed all German counter-attacks.

The machine gun arrangements of the 5th Australian Division – attacking on the left of 33rd Division – are also of considerable interest. The division set up separate groups to conduct SOS fire (four eight-gun batteries) and a creeping barrage (three eight-gun batteries). The latter group fired from positions in Glencorse Wood, a kilometre behind the front. The SOS fire group remained in action for eighty-five hours, firing 738,000 rounds against the area ahead of the Australian's final objective line. The group's telephone cable was cut, but it fired in response to SOS signals (distinctive red–green–yellow flares by this period). By great good fortune a telephonic link between the barrage group and the Divisional Machine Gun Officer was maintained throughout the sixty hours that the guns remained in action. This meant that, after the completion of their planned barrage, they were able to switch their fire to support 33rd Division's 98 Brigade, to their right, whose attack had become stalled. Captain Dunn, moving up with 2nd Royal Welsh Fusiliers in support of 98 Brigade, recalled benefiting from this support: 'It was as a rending of our part of the firmament. The staccato of the machine-guns filled the intervals of the larger reports of the shell-bursts, and the overhead rush of bullets through the near still, crisp air was like the whistle of a great wind.' Intelligence summaries after the battle reported that 'all prisoners agreed in saying that they had far more casualties from shrapnel and indirect machine gun fire than from high explosive'. In addition to the barrage groups, the Australians sent eight guns forward with each assaulting brigade. These proved crucial in consolidating the positions won during the attack. They were aided by the fact that 5th

Australian Division had ensured that its machine-gunners were familiar with the German MG08. A number of the latter were captured, and apparently proved of more utility than the Australian's own Vickers guns in repulsing counter-attacks, due to the large quantities of ammunition captured with them.

The Battle of Polygon Wood was one of a sequence of successful actions fought by General Plumer's Second Army. Plumer had also masterminded the Messines operation, and was the master of the 'bite and hold' offensive. It is probably no coincidence that his Army appears to have maintained a notably advanced attitude to machine-gunnery. The Germans meanwhile became desperate to find a way to stop Second Army's run of victories. Their problem stemmed from the fact that the limited objectives set by Plumer for his offensives ensured that the attackers were generally firmly dug in, with abundant supporting fire from artillery and machine guns, by the time the German counter-attack divisions arrived on the scene. It was therefore decided to thicken the front line with extra machine guns taken from rearward defensive positions and to closely support the front-line defenders with battalions sent forward from the counter-attack division. The machine guns of these battalions would also be placed in the forward defensive zone. By this means it was hoped to stall any attack in an area which would be well surveyed by the German artillery, and into which a concerted counter-attack could be mounted in due course. The immediate result in this change of tactics was a severe bloody nose during the Battle of Broodseinde (4 October 1917). This prompted a reversion to a more thinly held front line, although British intelligence reports suggested that greater numbers of machine guns were maintained there than had previously been the case. The Germans were spared further tactical contortions by the worsening conditions which brought the campaign to a muddy halt at Passchendaele. It is instructive, however, to note the importance accorded to the placement of machine guns during these tactical evolutions. One further notable aspect of German machine gun use at Ypres (and indeed in other parts of Flanders which had a high water table) was the use of reinforced concrete shelters to protect them from bombardment. Some of these pill boxes (as the British called them) featured embrasures through which the machine gun could be fired, but in most cases the gun was brought out to be fired from a platform at the rear of the shelter, or from a neighbouring shell-hole position.

The British were well aware of the tactical changes being made on the other side of the line. From a machine gun point of view the temporary presence of German counter-attacking forces so close to their forward positions increased the importance of Vickers guns sent forward for consolidation of newly won positions. Furthermore, according to the pamphlet SS201, it made 'an immediate response to SOS calls of critical importance'. So, tactical changes were being made by both sides throughout the battle. While 'Third Ypres' might have been fought in primordial conditions, it was in many respects a very modern battle.

Command and control

At the year's end, following the repulse of one further British attack at Cambrai and the alarming Italian collapse after Caporetto, both sides stood exhausted from the indecisive struggles of preceding nine months. The Allies looked to an infusion of new blood from the USA to turn the tide, but this would not come to fulfilment until late 1918. Meanwhile, the collapse of Russia gave the Germans access to reserves of manpower, which they made haste to use, in an attempt to win the war before the Americans could effectively intervene. As the new year dawned, the Allies awaited the inevitable assault.

This lull before the storm was actually an eventful period for the Machine Gun Corps. It witnessed a most important development: the creation of Machine Gun Battalions within divisions. According to the Official History, this move had been mooted for some time, but had been deferred until each Division had been provided with a fourth MG Company. Other sources make it evident that the matter was actually the subject of considerable debate at all levels of the Army. Until the reorganization took place, the fourth company was known as the Divisional Company, and remained at the disposal of its divisional HQ.

The creation of the battalion organization made perfect sense from the view of command and control, particularly given the primary importance accorded to barrage fire by this time. It also helped to ensure the flexible use of machine guns in support of the different brigades of the division, as well as cooperation with neighbouring formations. The latter was an essential requirement for the effective employment of machine guns in both attack and defence. The change to the new structure evidently took place over quite a long period. In most formations it occurred in March 1918 – this was certainly the case with the Canadian and Australian Corps. Some jumped the gun however. Hutchinson records that 33rd Division decided to adopt it as early as November 1917, in the wake of its experiences at Ypres – although this reorganization does not appear to have been ratified until the following February. The Canadians had, to an extent, also pre-empted the move by keeping their MG Companies within a loose semi-official battalion structure since the institution of the Canadian MGC in April 1917. By contrast, the MG Companies of Arthur Russell's 5th Division were not amalgamated until May 1918, although this delay might have been a result of the division's transfer to the Italian Front between December 1917 and April 1918.

Perhaps the most important feature of the new structure was that each division now had a Commander, Machine Gun Corps (CMGC). Previously the senior MGC officer had been known as the Divisional Machine Gun Officer (DMGO). This post first began to appear in mid-1917 – with the Second Army specifically calling for DMGOs to be appointed prior to Messines. The DMGO had been responsible for discipline, training and promotions among the men of his corps, but enjoyed no more than an advisory capacity with regard to the way in which his guns were employed. This was, militarily speaking, a nonsense. As Hutchinson testily remarked, 'in the Army one gives and receives orders, one neither gives or receives advice'. The handling of a division's machine guns was therefore at the whim of the divisional commander. Some would place great trust in their DMGO, whereas others would insist on the subordination of the MG Companies to the commanders of the brigades to which they were attached. The appointment of a CMGC ensured that machine gun schemes were planned at least on a divisional scale. They might indeed be orchestrated on a much grander scale, as the Battles of Vimy and Messines proved. This could be facilitated by the Corps Machine Gun Officer (CMGO), an appointment created in late 1916. At around the same time the Germans had established Regimental Machine Gun Officers – which might be seen as indicative of the contrast between the British 'top–down', separate corps, response to the machine gun issue and the German insistence on making machine guns organic to the infantry. In 1918 the post of Deputy Inspector of Machine Gun Units (DIMGU) was established in each Army and the post of CMGO was dispensed with. As before, the power and influence of these officers tended to be attendant upon the attitude towards machine-gunnery of the general officers who commanded their formations.

Apart from flexibility of deployment in combat, these changes addressed a more mundane issue. The perennial eagerness of individual officers to achieve promotion should never be overlooked as an influence on the composition of military formations. The institution of a battalion structure for the MGC went some way to addressing this matter; but evidently not far enough. To the frustration of its senior officers, the MGC was denied the complete chain of command that they desired – ideally perceived as culminating in an HQ MGC in France under the direction of a Major-General. Thus, officers such as George Lindsay (by this date installed as DIMGU at First Army) bewailed the fact that, in the absence of such a structure, officers tended to 'pass through' the corps on their way to more senior appointments.[17]

These changes were not achieved without opposition. From the outset, brigadiers had resisted the withdrawal of MG Companies from their control. This had been the reason for the 'advisory' role imposed upon the DMGOs.

Opinions evidently varied between formations. In September 1917 a report from Second Army advocated corps-level direction of machine gun operations, and recommended the use of the DMGO to organize the divisional schemes.[18] By contrast, a memorandum of the following month from the Guards Division suggested that any battalion organization should be limited to technical training and administration; with tactical training and handling remaining the responsibility of the brigadiers.[19] Even some officers within the MGC were wary of such radical changes. Colonel Hutchinson recalled that, even with the support of his divisional commander, it took him a whole eight hours to persuade the MGC company commanders of 33rd Division of the benefits of a change to a battalion structure.[20] He was also scandalized to find that, as late as May 1918, a III Corps memorandum was still able to question the command and control arrangements for its divisional machine guns.

The new MG battalions comprised four companies of sixteen guns each. This was evidently seen as the optimum size to control in battle. The Canadian Corps begged to differ. Its commander from June 1917, Sir Arthur Currie, took a keen interest in machine-gunnery and, on his own initiative, decided that his MG battalions should be stronger. By dint of requesting fifty of the 'best and brainiest' men from each infantry battalion in his corps, he created MG battalions of three large companies, disposing of thirty-two guns each. The principal tactical unit became the 'Battery' comprised of two four-gun sections. In the case of the British divisions, early 1918 was to see the importance of machine gun firepower enhanced for a very different reason. This was the decision, due to manpower shortages, to reduce the size of brigades from four battalions to three. The MG battalion therefore provided a significantly greater proportion of a division's firepower than the MG companies had formerly done.

Enter the USA

The year 1917 also witnessed a rather more obvious alteration to the Allied order of battle: namely the arrival of the first divisions of the American Expeditionary Force (AEF) on French soil. The machine gun complement of these divisions was, to say the least, striking. A fully equipped US infantry division could deploy as many as 260 machine guns (including those issued for anti-aircraft use) and over 1,000 automatic rifles. Each infantry regiment included a sixteen-gun machine gun company; each brigade boasted a sixty-four gun MG battalion and the division also contained a motorized MG battalion equipped with thirty-two guns. This astonishing level of equipment should of course be seen in the context of the huge size of American divisions – over 28,000 men. This compared with 11,800 for the divisions of the BEF,

11,400 for the French and just over 12,000 for those of the German Army. Nevertheless, it was a lavish scale of issue. Debate had taken place within the US Army regarding the creation of a separate machine gun branch, but this had been resolved decisively in favour of retention of machine guns within the existing arms of service.[21]

The actual equipment used was of interest, being more heterogeneous than that deployed by the other Allies. Even before he had designed the BAR, John M Browning had been developing a short-recoil operated machine gun. He recognized the shortcomings of his 'Potato-Digger' at an early stage, and came to the conclusion that gas operation was inferior to recoil operation in a weapon of this sort. His machine gun outwardly resembled other water-cooled guns of the era, but its system of operation was quite different. The bolt and barrel were locked together at the moment of firing by a transverse pin. As they recoiled rearwards, the pin was cammed downwards to unlock the breech. As part of the same movement a lever mechanism was activated to accelerate the rearward travel of the bolt. This system had the advantage of being simpler to manufacture and maintain than the Maxim system, while losing none of the latter's reliability. In fact, when tested in competitive trials, the Browning gun soundly beat all comers in terms of reliability. These included the Colt-made Model 1915 Vickers gun, which had already been accepted for service, but was not yet on issue to the Army. Plans were swiftly laid to put the Browning into production for the Army. Ironically, Colt, who held the sole rights to Browning's designs, were so deeply committed to the manufacture of the Vickers and the 'Potato-Digger' – the latter still being sold to the likes of Italy and Russia – that they were obliged to license production of Browning's machine gun and automatic rifle to other manufacturers.

Unfortunately, in common with the automatic rifle, the excellent Browning machine gun only arrived at the Front in time to see limited use before the Armistice. Its real triumphs were to come during the Second World War and the Korean War. The more usual machine gun equipment of the AEF was either the Vickers or the Hotchkiss. The first twelve US divisions to arrive in France were equipped with the Hotchkiss upon arrival. Divisions disembarking thereafter came already equipped with .30-calibre Colt Vickers guns, as these had begun to roll off the production line several months in advance of the Browning. Two exceptions were the 27th and 30th Divisions who, as they fought as part of British Fourth Army, received .303-inch Vickers guns through British channels. Not until the middle of October 1918 did the process of a general replacement of these guns by the Browning Model 1917 commence.

The AEF arrived in France with a tactical mindset which was strongly at variance with that which three years of industrial warfare had imposed upon the armies of its Allies. The US Army was wedded to the concept of the supremacy of the infantryman, armed with rifle and bayonet. The AEF's commander, General John Pershing, believed that the American soldier 'taught how to shoot, how to take advantage of the terrain, and how to rely upon hasty entrenchment, shall retain the ability to drive the enemy from his trenches and by the same tactics, defeat him in the open'.[22] He looked upon trench warfare as a tactical aberration into which his Allies had been drawn and looked to restore open warfare. He was supported in this by the official tactical doctrine of the US Army, which stressed 'self-reliant infantry, the rifle and bayonet, unlimited objectives and aggressiveness at all costs'.[23] Machine guns, according to the Field Service Regulations of 1914, which were still in force, were 'emergency weapons'. Despite the lessons learnt at such a bloody cost by those already at war, it was suggested that their 'effective use will be for short periods of time – at most but a few minutes – until silenced by the enemy'.

Dissenters from this tactical outlook existed. Machine-gunnery pioneer John Parker, now a lieutenant-colonel, went so far as to state, after visiting a French training centre that, 'the day of the rifleman is done. He was a good horse while he lasted, but his day is over.' Few in the US Army would have agreed with him; although some senior officers who had been sent to study French and British methods nurtured unspoken doubts about the tactics that their commander-in-chief intended them to employ. As it transpired, these overly aggressive, infantry-based tactics were to lead to severe casualties when the AEF went into action.

Chapter 6

From Triumph to Dissolution

Saul hath slain his thousands, and David his tens of thousands.

(1 Samuel 18: 7)

When the long awaited German offensive (or, rather, series of offensives) broke upon the Allied armies in Northern France during the spring of 1918, machine guns were once more in the forefront of the action. The causes of the failure of the British Fifth Army to hold the German *Michael* offensive remain the subject of debate to this day – a controversy in which machine guns are naturally involved. Some chose to criticize the performance of the MGC in a defensive role. Hutchinson was adamant that the German success was due to shortcomings in machine gun planning and a failure to implement the new battalion organization. Furthermore he stated that emplacements and ammunition supplies were found to be inadequate. A future Chief of the Imperial General Staff, Brigadier Edmund Ironside, confided to his diary that General Gough himself had been at fault for refusing to keep at least half of his machine guns out of front-line positions.[1] Of course, machine gun usage was only one element of the complex circumstances leading to the startling German break-in of 21 March 1918. Whatever the state of machine gun organization in the Fifth Army, it is clear that individual MGC units performed a vital and often self-sacrificing defensive role. A senior MGC officer, Colonel N K Charteris, later quoted General Ludendorff himself in support of this view. In a memorandum dated 30 March 1918 the author of *Michael* stated categorically that 'During the course of our offensive the principal resistance was offered by the machine gun nests distributed in depth.'[2] In this battle, more than any other, the men of the MGC earned their 'Suicide Club' tag. Bombarded by the high-explosive, shrapnel and gas cocktail of the German artillery 'concerto', attacked from the air, stalked by grenade-armed stormtroopers and made the special target of *minenwerfer*, their position was an unenviable one.

Nevertheless, properly handled and emplaced, machine guns could be sufficiently powerful to halt German attacks in their tracks. On 28 March the Germans launched their *Mars* offensive against the First Army, north of Arras. Among the formations opposing them was 56th Division. Their machine gun scheme was so well developed that it was later used as an example of the correct use of machine guns in the defence. The well-sited guns of 56th MG Battalion followed a complicated plan with interlocking fields of fire, supplemented by fire from the guns of neighbouring divisions, with Lewis guns covering areas of dead ground near the front line. Each battery of guns within range of the German front line was allocated both 'battle-lines' for direct fire and a target area for indirect SOS fire. As a result, despite a vicious bombardment and persistent attacks from the air, they played a major role in stopping an attack by greatly superior German forces. The only significant enemy lodgement in the British lines was gained in an area protected by its topography from being swept by Vickers fire. In other areas, particularly around the village of Gavrelle, very heavy casualties were meted out to the attackers. Many of the attackers had evidently not been inculcated with the latest German assault tactics; the Official History mentions them as being 'shoulder to shoulder' in Gavrelle. One captured German officer claimed that the machine guns had accounted for twelve officers of one regiment and twenty-four in another.[3] This is a good example of the efficacy of a properly established defensive position supported by an MG battalion. The new battalion organization also proved its worth in more fluid situations, where German break-ins had already occurred.

A prime example is provided by Hutchinson's own 33rd Battalion in its action near Méteren during the German *Georgette* offensive. On 12 April the Germans, having crossed the River Lys, were advancing north-west into the rear of the Second Army. At this juncture Hutchinson found himself using his battalion to hold the Germans on a low ridge south of Méteren, a village to the west of Baillieul. The feature is an insignificant one, but the good observation offered by its topography made it essential to hold it as a barrier against any German incursion into the Flanders plain to the north or towards the vital rail junction of Hazebrouck to the west. Hutchinson recorded the action in his memoir *Warrior*, which he later quoted in his work on machine guns. His account is breathlessly dramatic in tone (the fact that he supplemented his post-war income by writing thrillers might not be unconnected). Hutchinson brought his guns into action to stem the initial German assault: 'As they debouched we wracked them with machine-gun fire, and could observe enormous losses inflicted among them.' He then employed both his own battalion and a rag-bag of infantry units and stragglers to establish a proper line of defence until reinforcements (largely from 19 Brigade) could arrive. This involved, variously, the theft of two motor vehicles, sending drunken stragglers into suicidal counter-attacks ('they perished to a man'), turning his guns on British troops who abandoned their position and twice striking brother officers in front of their own men. Not for nothing was the composer Kenneth Alford (the creator of 'Colonel Bogey' and 'A Life on the Ocean Wave') later to write a march called 'The Mad Major' in Hutchinson's honour. However, the true significance of this action is not to be the found in the activities of one firebrand. Rather it lies in the fact that 33rd MG Battalion, with never so much as a brigade of infantry alongside, had held a three mile section of the line against overwhelming odds for almost a week. During this period the ridge was assaulted by elements of no less than ten German divisions plus (ironically, given the humble eminence concerned) the elite Alpenkorps. Naturally, the machine-gunners must share the credit with those who fought as infantrymen during this crisis. The historians of the 1st Queen's Regiment and the 5th/6th Cameronians make clear the toll exacted on the attackers by rifle and Lewis gun fire. However, it was 33rd MG Battalion which provided the basis of the defensive firepower throughout the action: an achievement that was recognized by a special order issued by IX Corps, describing the battle and stating that 'Throughout the operations the action of the 33rd Battalion Machine Gun Corps very materially assisted in preventing the enemy from capturing the Meteren position.'[4] The Official History's description of 33rd Division's defensive triumph states that 'According to all accounts it was the resolute handling of its machine gun battalion which contributed most to holding the Germans back from Meteren.' That this was also the view current at the time is confirmed by the fact that war correspondent Philip Gibbs reported that the machine-gunners 'fired so steadily into the waves of Germans that outside Meteren they wore out forty barrels'.

The same offensive provided a much-quoted example of machine gun use by a German assault unit, in an action fought by the 13th Reserve Infantry Regiment. The attacking battalion's sixteen-gun machine gun company swept the whole British position with the exception of a four metre gap, through which an entire battalion assaulted in single file. The progress of their attack was signalled by raising a helmet. Compared with contemporary British machine gun techniques this scheme was small-scale, clumsy and potentially dangerous to friendly troops. It would appear that the 'scientific' use of machine guns remained the preserve of the Maschinengewehr-Scharfschützen detachments, and that, despite their proven capacity for the aggressive use of light machine guns, the German shock troops were essentially more interested in getting up close with their *nahkampfmittel*: grenades, pistols and trench knives. For example, an abundance of the latter are listed among the equipment of four *Sturmkompagnien* (Assault Companies) of the 104th Infantry Regiment prior to an operation against French lines on 26 May 1918; but these companies possessed only three light machine guns and 1,750 rounds of belted machine gun ammunition between them.[5]

The MP18 mystery

One further weapon of close combat that has been associated with German assault troops is the MP18 submachine-gun. The German Army had been swift to perceive the potential for highly portable, short-range, automatic weapons and had begun experimenting with various concepts from 1915 onwards. In 1916 they had tested a fully automatic version of their 9mm Pistole 08 Lange (the long barrelled Luger pistol). However, it was found to be uncontrollable and to have too fast a rate of fire. Similar problems were found with a fully automatic 'carbine' version of the Mauser C96 pistol. Unlike the Austrians and the Italians, the Germans were not prepared to live with such faults. Finally, in 1917, the designer Hugo Schmeisser developed a promising machine pistol for the consideration of the military, and his design was taken up by the Theodor Bergmann Waffenbau. The history of this weapon, commonly known as the MP18, I (or, less regularly, as the Bergmann *Muskete*) is shrouded in mystery and has become the basis of not a little myth-making.

Schmeisser's design took the barrel of the long-barrelled Luger and combined it with a blowback action comprising a firing-pin riding inside a heavy bolt, which were driven into battery by a return spring. The weapon had a wooden stock and used the 32-round 'snail-drum' magazine already in production for use with P08 Lange. The peculiar magazine was the weak link in an otherwise workmanlike design. Nonetheless, if the weapon was going to be adopted, the use of existing components like the magazine and barrel was very much in its favour. However, the question of official adoption is one of the mysteries that dog the MP18. At least one expert has suggested that Schmeisser's gun was *never* officially taken into service.[6] The designation '18, I' may in fact relate to the Treasury budget which governed expenditure on such items.

In most armies however, official adoption was frequently only a rationalization of an issue that had already taken place. The MP18 certainly did see use in the field, whether adopted or not, but further mystery lies in the timing and scale of this use. The MP18 has frequently been seen as the very acme of the various weapons associated with the German stormtrooper – particularly in the context of the spring offensives of 1918. Sadly for this myth, the instruction manual for the MP18 was only produced in April 1918 and, while 'adoption' might follow issue, dissemination of instruction manuals invariably precedes it!

It appears clear that the MP18 only began to appear in the field from the summer of 1918 onwards. Examples with surviving provenance tend to have been captured in the last two months of the war. A rare reference to their issue appears in the history of the 104th Infantry Regiment, which describes them as a valuable supplement to automatic fire *against enemy assaults* (*Sturmabwehr*) in the 'last months'.[7]

The numbers of MP18s which saw combat were probably very limited. Much discussion has been devoted to the scale of this weapon's production – with figures of over 30,000 being quoted by some authorities. In fact, the serial numbers of surviving examples of this weapon *known to have been captured at the Front* do not appear to go beyond the 5,000 mark. The picture has been obscured by the fact that those MP18s issued after the war, to the police forces of the Weimar Republic, were either renumbered, or used a new range of numbers after being assembled from wartime parts. In at least some cases renumbering appears to have been achieved by the simple expedient of adding a digit in front of the original serial number – hence the existence of MP18s with numbers in the 30,000 range.

While it is certainly very likely that assault battalions got their hands on the new weapon, the official intention was to make a general issue of the MP18 to the infantry. Each infantry company was to have a seven-man *Maschinenpistole* team (one gunner and six ammunition carriers). As the meagre production figures imply, it did not prove possible to implement this plan before the Armistice. The terms of the subsequent peace treaty have been at the root of one further myth regarding the MP18. It is frequently repeated as fact that the Bergmann *Muskete* had so impressed the Allies during the 1918 campaign that they specifically banned its production and military issue. In fact no such prohibition appears in the terms of the Treaty of Versailles. Strict controls *were* placed on the production of firearms – principally by means of severely limiting the number of companies permitted to manufacture war materials – Bergmann was not among them. With regard to military issue, the numbers and types of weapons permitted to the 100,000-man German Army were carefully stipulated. There is no mention whatsoever made of machine pistols, although every other weapon type (apart from pistols) is listed – from cavalry carbines to 105mm Howitzers. Given the care that was taken to lay down such specific restrictions, it would appear that, far from having impressed the Allies, the MP18 had not really registered on their consciousness at all. The fact that they were still unconvinced of the utility of such weapons on the eve of the Second World War would also suggest that the impact of the MP18 on the fighting of 1918 was marginal.

Old solutions to new problems

British historians regularly (and rightly) complain that the great sequence of Allied victories in the last four months of the war constitute only a minor strand of the popular perception of the Great War, compared with the stale-mates of the Somme and 'Passchendaele'. From the point of view of machine-gunnery, however, it could also be said that the activities of machine-gunners constitute only a minor strand of historian's perception of the mechanism by which victory was achieved in 1918. It is plain enough that the Germans became ever more thoroughly reliant upon organic machine guns as the chief source of infantry firepower. On the other hand, our visualization of British and Dominion machine gun tactics is hazier. The dominant notion appears to be that the techniques developed during the period of trench warfare were no longer appropriate to the open warfare of 1918. This was certainly a view towards which I myself tended, prior to researching this book. There is, how-ever, plentiful evidence to suggest that quite the opposite was the case.

First of all the concept of 'open' warfare is a relative one. The advances made were huge compared with those achieved during 1915 and 1917 and often involved movement across open country. However the major engagements which took place were normally characterized by Allied troops driving the Germans from prepared defensive positions. Here machine gun barrage fire obviously had a part to play. Meanwhile the MGC had already given thought to the employment of its guns in more mobile conditions of warfare. The pamphlet SS201 had identified the challenge which might be presented by open warfare, stating that: 'The development of rapidly produced barrage fire by organized machine gun batteries will be an essential feature of any suc-cessful effort at pushing forward under conditions of open warfare.' George Lindsay insisted that machine-gunners should be prepared 'not only to give direct covering fire during the mobile phases, but to be able quickly to provide Indirect Barrages for attacks of a "set-piece" nature, whether they are on a large or small scale'.[8] He also voiced his opinion that 'The more open fighting becomes, the greater is the need for over-head covering fire from the Machine Gun Batteries under central control.'

An informed reading of the evidence relating to the battles of the 'Hundred Days' reveals innumerable examples of such barrages. Pride of place among these sources must go to the *Narrative of Machine Gun Operations. IV Army. April–November 1918*, which was written by the DIMGU, Fourth Army, Colonel N K Charteris. This Army had been formed from the remains of the shattered Fifth Army in the spring of 1918, and was the most southerly of the BEF's five armies during the remaining months of the war. The account is replete with all manner of useful information but, above all, gives details of the many barrages fired by Fourth Army's machine-gunners during this period.

Prominent among the constituent parts of Fourth Army was the Australian Corps. One of this elite formation's most famous actions was fought at Hamel on 4 July 1918. In the course of this action, 4th Australian Division was supported by its own machine guns and also those of the three other Australian divisions. A barrage was fired involving 111 of these guns, carefully co-ordinated with the artillery barrage. Thus machine guns played their part in the success of what has been justly celebrated as an early example of true 'combined arms' warfare – expertly orchestrated by the Australian Corps commander, Lieutenant-General John Monash.

Another battle in which the Australian Corps was to play an important role was that of Epehy on 18 September 1918, when the BEF broke into the so-called 'Hindenburg Outpost Line' (which was in fact the British trench system of 1917 'turned' to become the most westerly element of the *Siegfried Stellung*). Charteris offers two very eloquent reports gathered by Australian machine-gunners regarding the effectiveness of their barrages on that day:

> The infantry spoke highly of the support afforded to them by the machine gun barrages, both by initial barrages and by those on the second objectives. As regards the initial barrage the 45th Australian Infantry Battalion stated that during the approach of the first objective they found a large number of dead Germans, one lot of thirty in particular, killed by bullets, apparently while running away. Three prisoners belonging to the 58th Silesian Regiment (one of whom was a machine gunner) stated that almost all the casualties around them were from machine-gun fire, and that the machine gun barrage itself had amazed them.
>
> As regards the barrage on the second objective, the value of heavy concentrations of machine-gun fire on selected areas during the advance was emphasized by the infantry. Enemy machine guns were found in the trenches with their barrel casings pierced and their crews killed by machine-gun fire. Prisoners stated that they were unable to serve their guns on account of the severity of our machine-gun fire.

Also involved in this operation was the British 74th Division. This division formed part of III Corps. The heretical views of the staff of this corps regarding MG battalions, which Hutchinson later decried, appear not to have undermined the effectiveness of their barrage fire, which was described by one infantryman as: 'like the tearing of a huge sheet of calico or the firing of a million rifles'.

The detailed accounts given by Charteris of Fourth Army machine gun barrages continue right up until the last days of the war – with detailed maps to accompany them which show complex mixtures of precisely timed creeping and standing barrages – generally fired on a divisional level. Examples include barrages fired by 50th Division at Le Cateau on 17 October, and another fired by 6th and 46th Divisions at Vaux Andigny on 21 October.

Lest the impression is formed that such activities were restricted to the Fourth Army, there are examples of barrages fired elsewhere in the Front – most notably by the Canadian Corps in the First Army. On 27 September, a major Canadian barrage was fired in support of their crossing of the Canal du Nord. This was conducted by twenty-four batteries (192 guns), which were divided into subgroups that fired creeping barrages moving at varying speeds according to local tactical requirements. The chronicler of the Canadian 'Emma Gees', Lieutenant-Colonel Grafton, recorded that 320,000 rounds were fired and 'a new adaptability had been marked up for machine gunnery in a barrage role'. The Canadian Corps was also responsible for what might have been the last serious machine gun barrage of the war (seventy-two guns), fired during 4th Canadian Division's attack at Valenciennes, on 2 November 1918.

Mobility

Naturally the mobile tactical environment of the Hundred Days created many new challenges for troops and commanders conditioned to the positional warfare that had previously prevailed – machine-gunners were no exception to this. Nevertheless, it can be argued that machine guns were reasonably mobile: certainly more so than artillery. This was undoubtedly the reason that 'on many occasions', as Charteris put it, infantry attacks were made with machine gun support alone. The main problem was ensuring a sufficient supply of ammunition. At Hamel the Australians had enterprisingly arranged for the dropping of small arms cartridges from aircraft. 114,000 rounds were dropped in response to a white 'V' spread by the machine-gunners on the ground. Normally however, it was the 'fighting limbers' that were the key to mobility, and which generally permitted the machine-gunners to keep pace with the advancing infantry while ensuring that they were themselves sufficiently stocked with ammunition. When operating among woods, buildings and hedges, it was found that limbers could sometimes be brought safely within 200m of the machine gun position. Hutchinson even went so far as to expedite the advance through the Forêt de Mormal by driving some limbers into a river to form a makeshift causeway. He was also an advocate of the 'Half Limber', wherein the front part of the limber was detached from the rear – increasing mobility but reducing ammunition capacity. However, Charteris was firmly of the opinion that 'Half limbers should rarely be used.'

Some machine-gunners did not have to rely upon animal power for their mobility. Brutinel's Canadian Motor Machine Gun Brigade (CMMGB) had been able to do little more than provide barrage support for the infantry prior to 1918. However, when the Fifth Army was in retreat during March 1918, the Brigade was sent off 'into the blue' (as Grafton put it) to stem any potential German breakthroughs. With its utility in 'open' warfare established, this formation was expanded and split into a 1st and 2nd CMMGB during the summer of 1918. These new formations first saw action during the Battle of Amiens. According to Charteris, who saw these truck-borne machine-gunners in action there when they were attached to Fourth Army, they drove 'clean through' the enemy lines, 'dropping guns and teams where required as they went'. In addition, the CMMGB still deployed armoured trucks of the type originally purchased by Brutinel. These were 30cwt vehicles manufactured by the Autocar Company of Pennsylvania, and fitted with armour-plate by the Bethlehem Steel Corporation of the same state. The armour enclosed the engine and provided open-topped protection for the cab and two Vickers gun crews who operated their weapons from the rear bed of the truck. Brutinel once again took personal charge of this mobile force during the Hundred Days and augmented it with a wireless section, two sections of 6-inch mortars mounted on flatbed trucks and the Canadian Corps Cyclist Battalion. At various points he also enjoyed the support of a Field Artillery Battery and the Canadian Light Horse. The officer commanding First Army, General Horne, was evidently impressed with this arrangement, as he permitted his DIMGU – namely George Lindsay – to raise a similar formation. This was based around two truck-borne MG battalions of thirty-two guns each, and eight armoured cars.

Not surprisingly, as the fluidity of operations increased, machine-gunners frequently found themselves in positions which would have been hard to imagine only a few months earlier. For a start, those guns selected as 'forward' (rather than barrage) guns frequently found themselves able engage 'targets of opportunity', such as enemy artillery, with direct fire. As Charteris pointed out, traditional machine gun lore had strongly advised against engaging in a duel with artillery, but 'on the contrary, no opportunity of doing so should be lost'. Forward guns were also regularly called upon by the infantry at this period to neutralize German machine guns – a task which had previously fallen largely to trench mortars, artillery or, indeed, to the infantry themselves. Charteris also gives more than one example of machine gun officers taking control of infantry units in certain situations. One such was Lieutenant Hoff of

46th MG Battalion, at Montbrehain on 3 October. He rallied a group of infantrymen who had been forced to retreat by a German counter-attack. After setting up the guns of his section to provide direct overhead covering fire, he led the infantry into an attack which, with the aid of a tank (although this was swiftly put out of action), restored the situation. Nor was it only the forward guns that got mixed up in infantry combat. In the Hindenburg Outpost Line on 17 September, an Australian machine gun officer was setting up his guns for a barrage when: 'A German officer came out of a trench and shouted "Mercy, kamerad, I can't get my men to fight and I want to surrender"'. The Australian machine gun officer replied "All right, I won't hurt you" and went on with the job of getting his guns into position for the next barrage.'

Vanguards and rearguards

The changing face of warfare at this period necessitated the formation of vanguards to probe the positions of the enemy and ascertain whether he intended to stand or retreat. The dominant position now held by the machine gun as a provider of firepower meant that these vanguards had, of necessity, to include an MGC element. In 55th Division (First Army) special all-arms groups were formed to perform this function for each brigade. They consisted of the following:

1 MG Company;
1 Troop of Cavalry;
1 Battery of 18-Pounder field guns;
1 Section of 4.5-inch howitzers;
1 Section of trench mortars on carriages extemporized from GS
    wagons;
1 Section Royal Engineers;
First Aid detachment;
Investigation party to check enemy positions and dugouts for booby
    traps.[9]

Dunn records that, from August onwards, 38th Division (Third Army) attached an MG section to each infantry battalion. In Fourth Army the general procedure was for MG companies to support divisional vanguards with two sections 'up' and the other two sections 1,000–1,500 yards to the rear. The forward guns could be brought into action to neutralize enemy machine guns, but the main purpose of the MG company was to protect the open flanks of the vanguard and defend against counter-attacks. Even in these circumstances, the MG companies could be called upon to mount indirect shoots when potential centres of German resistance were identified. It is interesting to note that such arrangements were not entirely novel. During the German withdrawal to the *Siegfried Stellung* in March 1917, British Fifth Army had created all-arms 'Advance Guards' to keep in touch with the enemy.[10] Moreover, what were the arrangements in 38th Division other than a return to the organization of 1914?

Thus, faced with a new form of warfare, the MGC continued to rely upon its proven tactics wherever possible. Even when senior commanders felt the need to create specialized *ad hoc* formations, these tended to represent a reversion to tried and trusted methods which had been used earlier in the war. Even the use of motor machine guns was merely the fulfilment of tactical planning for open warfare which had begun as early as 1915.

What of the German machine-gunners during this period? All sources indicate that now, more than ever before, they formed the core of German firepower and invariably constituted the spine of any defensive position. At Amiens on 8 August, as Bill Rawling notes, the main German defence was a 'vast number of machine guns hidden in great depth'. Another historian of the Canadian Corps has suggested that the arrival of new Maschinengewehr-Scharfschützen detachments at the Front posed a greater threat than the appearance of new divisions of infantry. Although the overall quality of the German Army dwindled, these elite machine-gunners proved 'remarkably cohesive'.[11] As the Hundred Days progressed, the Official History records that 'In every case it was the enemy machine guns which, if they did not entirely stop, at least slowed up the advance. To the end the machine gun was the hard core of the resistance.' By November, Arthur Russell was to receive the following impression:

> If any Boche infantry were with their machine-gun teams they were most inactive – no hostile rifle shots rang out; no trench mortars crashed into our positions; and none of their all too familiar stick-bombs were thrown at us. German artillery had now stopped completely; undoubtedly they were rapidly pulling their guns out of action, and out of reach of the victorious Allied Armies ... It was as though the last hours of the Great War were developing into a duel between the Machine Gun Organizations of the opposing armies.

So, as the War approached its end, German machine-gunners maintained their splendid reputation. Meanwhile, however, the German Army as whole was indubitably in decline. Machine gun nests might well have provided a defensive framework or an effective rearguard where circumstances demanded. Unfortunately for the German machine-gunners, the Army as a whole was now prey to the debilitating effects of four years of war on multiple fronts. Operationally it was also suffering the pernicious after-effects of having rammed itself into a strategic cul-de-sac earlier in the year. Relying upon machine-gunners to stem the Allied advance while other units melted away around them may have been effective, but it was a policy of desperation.

The AEF in combat

As previously outlined, the American Expeditionary Force was, at least officially, wedded to the concept of gaining victory through the élan and aggression of its riflemen. Like the Armies of the Great Powers in 1914, it was to find that such tactics were supreme consumers of soldiers' lives. For instance, at Soissons between 18 and 21 July 1918, troops of the 1st and 2nd Divisions 'advanced in steady lines across open wheat fields as German machine-gunners shot them down'.[12] However, not all American commanders shared Pershing's tactical outlook, and more sophisticated tactics were already to be found in use within the AEF during the summer of 1918. These were, perhaps, most noticeably evident in the way in which machine guns were employed.

It is for example clear that the use of machine gun barrage fire was widespread. The US 1st Division, whose machine-gunners had been trained by the French, deployed three barrage groups (of between six and twenty-four guns) during the first American offensive operation of the war at Cantigny, on 28 May 1918. The National Guardsmen of 26th Division also employed barrage fire. This was the result of a visit paid by their commander, Major General Clarence R Edwards, to 51st Highland Division in October 1917 when, he wrote, nothing 'made such an impression on me in my visit … as the machine gun barrage'.[13] Some criticism was subsequently directed at the performance of 26th Division and it is interesting to note that its machine gun barrage work was brought up to scratch by the expedient of installing Colonel John Parker as DMGO. He personally assured the accuracy of his gunners' work by driving around in his car beneath the arc of their overhead fire.

It is evident, nevertheless, that the US divisions developed their machine gun tactics at varying paces. For example, the 2nd Division notably failed to integrate machine gun fire into their plan of attack for the Aisne–Marne offensive of 18–19 July 1918. However, less than a month later, at St Mihiel, their orders incorporated an annex devoted entirely to the use of machine guns – both for close support and in a barrage role. Some US Army commanders were greater enthusiasts of automatic firepower than others. Prominent among the former was Major-General Charles P Summerall of 1st Division and, subsequently, V Corps. He ordered a massive barrage by V Corps machine-gunners during the Meuse–Argonne offensive in November 1918. One of the attacking divisions was supported by no less than 255 machine guns.

Summerall was also an advocate of the use of machine guns in direct support of attacks. In this he was aided by the generous scale of machine gun issue within the US divisions. Indeed, it appears to have become the practice throughout the AEF for barrage fire to be conducted by the Brigade Machine Gun Battalions, while the Regimental Machine Gun Companies provided direct fire support. The experience gained with machine guns in combat led many in the US Army to the same conclusions as their British counterparts. The commander of 29th Division, Major-General Charles G Morton, lecturing in 1919, echoed the British pamphlet SS192 when he stated that 'this war has disposed of the old theory that machine guns have their greatest use in defense ... their greatest use is in the offensive'.[14]

Towards modern warfare

By 1918, particularly on the Western Front, each of the warring nations had arrived at a system of small-unit tactics based on the firepower of automatic rifles or light machine guns. Development of these tactics was to continue during that decisive year, as trench warfare gave way to more mobile operations. The tactical successes of the German spring offensives were at least partially due to the employment of a set of offensive tactics that had been pioneered by special assault battalions and refined over the preceding eighteen months. These were summarized in the instructional pamphlet *Der Angriff in Stellungskrieg* (The Attack in Position-Warfare). This made clear the role to be played by light machine guns: 'Numerous machine guns must be attached from the very first to the troops leading the assault in order that, where there is a check, they may be available to cover the advance of riflemen and bombers.' Thus it was intended that the assault should be carried forward by grenade-armed shock troops, with the machine guns coming into play when the attack was held up. This did not necessarily mean that the light machine-gunners lagged behind the advance. Indeed they often deployed ahead of the main body, the better to develop their covering fire. This aggressive use of light machine guns impressed the British, who recommended the adoption of similar tactics for the Lewis gun, in an amendment to their pamphlet SS197, published in June 1918.

However, like the Allies before them, the Germans found that they now had a recipe for tactical success, but they were still unable to achieve their strategic goal: i.e. a decisive breakthrough. When, from July 1918, the bankruptcy of Ludendorff's unfocused strategy became evident, and the Allies turned once again to the offensive, light automatics came once more to the fore. In the British and Dominion forces, the Lewis gun was to acquire even greater significance than before. The ever improving availability of Lewis guns facilitated the issue of thirty-six per battalion. This was sufficient for an issue of two per platoon, plus four held at the battalion HQ for anti-aircraft purposes. Meanwhile, manpower shortages meant that infantry battalions were being reduced in size. The smaller battalion necessitated a reorganization of platoons into a Lewis gun section and two rifle sections. In July 1918 the specialist bombing and rifle grenade sections were officially abolished; but this would appear to have been no more than a confirmation of a movement towards a more integrated platoon structure, which had already occurred in the field. Thus the Lewis gun became, if not the dominant infantry weapon, at least the first among equals. The BEF's Director of Training, Lieutenant-General Sir Ivor Maxse, stated that 'A platoon without a Lewis gun is not a platoon at all.' Meanwhile the new commander of the Australian Expeditionary Force, Lieutenant-General John Monash, professed himself unworried by manpower shortages, as long as enough Lewis guns were present to maintain a battalion's firepower.

Not surprisingly, given the immense casualties suffered in the course of their unsuccessful offensives, the Germans too began to suffer shortages of personnel. As infantry companies dwindled in size, they frequently lacked the manpower to carry more than four LMGs into action.[15] Within platoons the LMG was deployed in a nine-man squad or *Gruppe*, comprising the squad leader, the four-man gun team and four riflemen to protect them. The platoon would also include pure rifle squads and, possibly, a specialist assault squad. During 1918, the ever-increasing availability of the MG08/15 encouraged the reorganization of platoons into *Einheitsgruppe*. These were squads of a universal composition, all based around an LMG team.

The Germans invariably displayed a good deal of flexibility in the composition of their small units, which could be put together on a 'mix and match' basis to suit the task in hand. However, as with other armies, it was the introduction of the light automatic that facilitated these developments. German doctrine made a clear distinction between a unit's firepower (*feuerkraft*) and 'striking power' (*stosskraft*). From 1917 onwards, it was the MG08/15 that became the supreme provider of the former in infantry platoons – a development which was confirmed by the structural changes of 1918. A parallel reorganization took place in the French Army in October 1918, when platoons were re-organized into three *Groupes de Combat*, each based around a six-man CSRG team. Meanwhile the Americans too were learning the vital importance of the automatic rifle. Their leading proponent of automatic firepower, General Summerall, asserted that the rifle was 'greatly inferior in value' to the automatic rifle, and directed that every infantryman should be trained to shoot the latter if necessary. He further instructed that every rifleman going into the attack in his 1st Division should carry a CSRG magazine, to prolong the functionality of the automatic rifles.[16]

Thus, by final months of the war, light machine guns and machine rifles were no longer a novelty and, instead of being placed in specialized subunits, were now becoming integral to each squad or section of the infantry of the major combatants. The introduction of light machine guns and 'machine-rifles' had, in fact, transformed the tactics of those lucky enough to be issued with them in quantity. They were to prove a key element in the increasingly sophisticated combined-arms tactics used by both sides as the war reached its climax. These weapons, and the tactics that evolved to accompany them, were a true innovation of the Great War.

Machine guns in general had of course been around for almost thirty years by 1914, and were an established part of every army at the outbreak of war. Nevertheless, nobody had predicted the extent to which they would come to dominate the battlefield. On the Marne in 1914 the Germans had deployed an average of 3.5 machine guns per kilometre of front. In July 1918, in the Soissons–Reims area, the density of machine guns was 31.5 per kilometre.[17] Most German divisions could, by this time, boast over 100 machine guns and around 180 light machine guns. This extraordinary growth in machine gun use was, of course, replicated in the other armies on the Western Front, as well as in those of Italy and Austria-Hungary. The latter surrendered 43,777 machine guns at the war's end and an Austrian tactical manual of April 1918 stated that 'grenade launchers, mortars and particularly machine guns are the mainstays of the infantry firefight'.[18]

To complete this overview of levels of machine gun use at the war's end: some further figures. France had 43,000 machine guns on issue at the end of the war – having produced 88,000 since August 1914. Vickers produced over 75,000 machine guns during the war and, by November 1918 the MGC had swollen in size to almost 120,000 men. As we have seen, production of light machine guns and automatic rifles greatly exceeded even these impressive figures and light automatics were central to every infantry platoon on the Western Front. Merely quoting numbers does not do justice to the importance that machine guns had attained by 1918. Taken as a whole, however, the preceding chapters should leave the reader in no doubt of their rise to be the pre-eminent provider of infantry firepower.

The great British machine gun controversy

As the Armistice of 11 November 1918 brought an end to the most destructive war that the world had yet known, all parties had come to accept that machine guns constituted the indispensable core of infantry firepower. Nevertheless, in the British and Dominion armies controversy reigned with regard to the correct methods by which to apply it. The infantry had never quite become reconciled to their loss of control of the Vickers gun and, while many officers appreciated the support of machine gun barrages, others felt that the firepower was more effective if aimed directly by guns in close support of their own men. Meanwhile there were some in the artillery – the arm which had risen to a position of vast power and influence during the course of the war – who resented the activities of the 'Little Gunners' and went out of their way to dismiss them as ineffective.

The apparent difficulty of assessing the effects of indirect machine gun fire formed a major element of this inter-corps controversy. Unlike artillery fire, it could not be observed from the air, nor did it send plumes of earth and smoke into the air when it struck home. Nevertheless, and perhaps surprisingly, it was frequently possible to observe the strike of machine gun fire, even in the thick of battle. Early in the war the German expert von Merkatz had written that:

> While before the war, I was of the opinion that the machine-gun sheaf [i.e. cone of fire] would often disappear in the volume of the infantry sheaf and of striking shrapnel so that it could not be observed, this was not substantiated in the war. The machinegun sheaves could generally be recognized even in the most intense firing of our own troops. In battle, the difficulty of observation lies not so much in the visibility of the striking projectiles as in the invisibility of the targets.[19]

The British pamphlet SS201 made specific reference to the fact that the bullet strikes of a machine gun barrage fired at Shrewsbury Forest in the Ypres Salient on 20 September 1917 were clearly visible. This event occurred during a dry period; mud obviously made observation more difficult.

This fact did nothing to quiet the debate which raged about indirect fire. The reluctance of many regimental officers to acknowledge the effectiveness of barrages is clear from Dunn's comments regarding bullets being wasted on patches of ground and his jibe about 'the jawbone of an ass'. Nonetheless, his diary is actually unusual in alluding to the support provided machine gun barrages at all – they seldom receive a mention in regimental histories or infantry battalion war diaries. Even among the advanced thinkers of the Canadian Corps a simmering row persisted regarding the effectiveness of unobserved machine gun fire: the chief antagonists being Brutinel and the Corps artillery commander Andrew McNaughton.[20]

The proponents of the machine gun barrage were swift to counter this scepticism with reports from prisoners regarding the effectiveness of the barrages which they had to endure. These reports were evidently plentiful, although it should be remembered that newly captured men are generally inclined to tell their captors whatever they think they wish to hear. It is interesting to note that, in the wake of the Canadian barrage fired at Mont Huoy, near Valenciennes on 2 November 1918, McNaughton compiled his own report from prisoner interviews, which suggested that the artillery, rather than the machine guns, had provided the most effective element of the barrage. This survey is however put into perspective if we take into account the fact that, such were the material resources of the Allies at this time, McNaughton was able to deluge the German positions with over 2,000 tons of shells – roughly equivalent to the quantity expended during the entire Boer War![21]

Another brilliant artillerist, Sir Herbert Uniacke, gave a very curious appraisal of British machine-gunnery, which is quoted by his fellow gunners Bidwell and Graham:

> In the first place the Germans in 1918 provided their own machine gun barrage from their forward troops which was successful. Yet our own counterattacks were very often stopped by counter machine-gun fire. The whole machine gun question needs to be closely examined to discover wherein our inferiority lies, whether in the number of guns employed, the training of the companies, the technical and tactical training of the officers, or any other cause. The matter is very important; it has been our chief weakness throughout the war.

This outburst is of interest less for the quality of its forensic rhetoric than for what it tells us of writer's perception of his subject matter. Nobody would dispute the effectiveness of German machine gun fire. However, Uniacke might have reflected that the neutralization of this fire was not the chief role of the MGC, but rather the preserve of Lewis gun and rifle grenade teams, trench mortars and, ultimately, the field–gunners of his own corps. His complaint also betrays an ignorance of barrage fire in the sense that officers of the MGC would have understood it. Unfortunately this is a typical example of the compartmentalized thinking which, despite all the technical and tactical progress, still prevailed in the British Army at the close of the war. Reference has already been made to a contrasting parallel, in the form of Hutchinson's ignorance of tactical training for Lewis guns. This compartmentalization was a symptom of unfortunate traits which lay deeply embedded in the psyche of the British Army. Tim Travers has alluded to the 'Hidden internal war', which 'pitted the power of prewar ideas and the power of the *prewar army structure* [emphasis added], against the encroaching reality of a "modern" technological war'. A French interpreter who worked with the BEF for three years gave an interesting outsider's view: 'The British army has improved a lot, but yet there is still much to improve. An Englishman is not prepared to learn from another, and only wants to learn through his own experience, and hence many thousands of lives and lots of money are wasted and precious time is lost.'[22]

Any impartial reading of the available evidence must surely lead to an acceptance of the effectiveness of the techniques developed by the MGC – although we might stop short of Colonel Luxford's opinion that 'The British machine gun, its uses and its tactics developed wonderfully, and completely overshadowed the German machine guns from June, 1917, until the end of the war.' Whether in grand set-piece battles or in the course of the victorious advances of the 'Hundred Days' the MG barrage reigned supreme, and it was generally fired with considerable effect. However this assessment is the result of *ex post facto* analysis. In the heat of battle the contribution of the MGC must have been difficult for others to perceive – be they the eighteen-year-old conscript advancing into the attack, or the Brigadier General Royal Artillery at divisional HQ. In 1918 British infantry might expect to have the support of an artillery creeping barrage, smoke shells and, possibly, tanks and ground-attack aircraft. All of these are far more noticeable on the battlefield than a machine gun barrage. Herein might lie another key to failure of the Army as a whole to embrace the concept of a specialist corps of machine-gunners. The inability of the MGC to gain universal acceptance of its techniques and their efficacy was to cost it dear.

In 1918, the future of the MGC and the continued organization of machine guns into battalion-sized formations were by no means taken for granted. A survey was conducted by the committee charged with planning the *post-bellum* army, which asked a number of questions regarding machine gun organization. Copies of George Lindsay's answers to Papers 'E: Machine Guns with a Division' and 'K: Corps and Army Machine Guns', are preserved. Not sur- prisingly this most enthusiastic of machine-gunners took the opportunity to go further than the contemporary status quo, and recommend that MG battalions be expanded to comprise ninety-six guns, and that extra battalions should be available at Corps and Army level. Evidently the majority of officers did not share his vision and, most importantly, neither did those in charge at the War Office for, in 1922, the MGC was disbanded. The Corps' memorial to its 12,498 wartime dead stands at Hyde Park Corner. It is a statue of the Boy David, and the biblical quotation on its plinth makes not only grim reference to the wartime effectiveness of the MGC, but also hints at how members of the Corps envisaged themselves within the hierarchy of the Army: 'Saul hath slain his thousands, and David his tens of thousands.'

The circumstances of the MGC's disappearance from the British Army's order of battle are curious, particularly when compared with the anguish which has invariably accompanied the disbandment or amalgamation of county regiments (themselves, as Gary Sheffield likes to point out, akin to the 'traditional' Christmas – merely an invention of the late nineteenth century). The dispersal of the MGC's officers to other units meant that no proper history of the corps was ever written. The Corps' mess silver was melted down to make a font for the Royal Memorial Chapel at Sandhurst. The fact that the MGC's history was erased in this manner has caused dark suggestions to be made about the role which inter-corps rivalry might have played in the decision. The main impetus behind the disbandment of the MGC was undoubtedly financial, but was there malice in the decision to let the axe fall on this new Corps? This might be difficult to prove and circumstantial evidence suggests otherwise. It was hardly unknown in the inter-war British Army for decisions on organization and equipment to default back to the *status quo ante bellum*. Furthermore, with the Army returning to its pre-war role as a sort of colonial gendarmerie, and with no European war imminent, the War Office can perhaps be forgiven for seeing no vital role for a separate corps of machine-gunners. When the time came for massed Vickers guns to open fire once more, the face of warfare itself had changed.

Epilogue

The Machine Gun Legacy – Reality and Myth

Prior to the Great War, if any soldier had suggested any one of the following propositions he would have been damned eternally: that cavalry would have no role in modern European warfare; that controlled rifle-fire would disappear and machine guns and automatic rifles take its place; that bayonets would be preferred as toasting-forks and superseded by bombs as weapons; that troops could face 50 per cent casualties and more and yet go on – yet these things happened. (Lt Col G S Hutchinson)

The armies were held fast in the grip of Hiram Maxim. The history of the years that followed is one of ceaselessly renewed frontal on-slaughts on entrenched lines held in reality by machine guns, if nominally by infantry. (Capt B H Liddell Hart)

When we consider machine guns (and indeed small arms in general) today, we are looking from a perspective in which the weapon system is effectively at the end of its cycle of development. With the exception of the possible future introduction of caseless ammunition, there is little that can still be done to improve the battlefield effectiveness of firearms. We are now standing at the end of a period of evolution which gained momentum during the late nineteenth century and which was given further impetus by the World Wars. The basic varieties of military firearm currently in use have been with us for some decades now. This makes it all too easy to seize the benefit of hindsight to criticize the perceived failings of our forebears. The armies of the First World War have long been the subject of such criticism, and certain historians have been quick to castigate the military establishments of the combatants for their short-sightedness or tardiness in adopting new technology. At the same time, firearms specialists have excoriated them for adopting weapons which do not meet what are, in fact, anachronistic standards of performance and reliability.

I would argue, and would hope that this book makes clear, that the First World War saw designers striving to deliver the best weapons possible within the technological limitations of the day, and governments attempting to produce as many of these weapons as the constraints of wartime production permitted.

Military men of all nations were, nonetheless, certainly guilty of failing to predict the effect that modern firepower would have. This failure could be attributed to the incomplete and potentially misleading lessons learnt from the Boer War and Russo-Japanese War. However, it was doubtless also the outcome of the fact that military thinkers were unwilling to admit that defensive firepower could be so powerful as to negate all their strategic and tactical plans and render their armies all but impotent. Indeed the only man to give public voice to such fears was a civilian, the Polish banker I S Bloch; whose book, *Is War Impossible?* offered that very hypothesis. Had the potential effect of quick-firing artillery and machine guns been fully comprehended, we can be sure that the war plans of the Great Powers, and perhaps even their attitude to war as a means to resolve political conflicts, would have been very different. Sadly it seems that it was necessary to experience the bloodletting of 1914 before the realities of modern industrialized warfare were driven home. Nevertheless, once these realities had been made manifest, it is clear that all the combatants showed an eagerness to adopt new technologies and develop new tactics to overcome the deadlock.

It is in this context that the rise of automatic firepower should be viewed. From being an adjunct to the *feuerkraft* of the infantry, the machine gun evolved into the essential basis of that firepower. The Great War witnessed the evolution of 'scientific' machine-gunnery, an amalgam of tactics and techniques undreamt-of by most pre-war soldiers and scarcely understood or even known of today. It was of the course the British Army and Imperial contingents who took this process the furthest, by establishing machine-gunners as an arm-of-service in their own right. Light machine guns and 'machine rifles' were a completely novel development of the First World War. Their importance lay not so much in their own capabilities, which were limited by the technology of the day, as in their revolutionary effect on small-unit organization and tactics. In 1914 it was hoped to suppress the enemy's fire by the controlled fire of companies of riflemen. By 1918 most armies were basing their tactics on the platoon, consisting of two or more subunits based around light automatic weapons. Once the deadlock on the Western Front had been established, the warring armies strained every sinew to break it. Far from being dismissed by a hidebound military hierarchy, any new tactical concept or technological advance which might facilitate a breakthrough was seized upon, and the Great War became a ferment of military innovation. Just as its political outcome set the strategic and diplomatic agenda for the remainder of the twentieth century, the tactical concepts developed in its course created a battlefield environment for subsequent 'conventional' wars, which would still be recognizable as late as the 1982 Falklands Conflict.

This crucial reality has not been accorded the recognition it deserves in most traditional histories of the First World War. In the past, it proved all too easy to follow the conventional line that the war was characterized by doomed soldiers sent 'over the top' into hopeless attacks by bumbling 'cavalry generals' from the safety of their 'chateaux'. This view retains a surprisingly tenacious hold on the public imagination – one which is unlikely to be broken by either this book or any other work of history. Notwithstanding this sad fact, many studies of recent years have attempted to shed light on the tactical advances which occurred during the Great War. Unfortunately, some of these appear to have at their heart an urge to prove the excellence of one protagonist at the expense of the others. This is all too frequently based on a close reading of the tactical manuals of the chosen 'innovators' coupled with an ignorance of the tactical precepts of those unfavourably contrasted with them. I would contend, and would submit the contents of the preceding chapters as evidence, that *all* armies adopted the tactics and equipment best suited to their aims – at least insofar as was possible within the constraints of procurement and production. For example, the British were impelled to develop machine gun barrage fire as a way of making effective use of machine guns in the course of offensive operations (whether as a support to the assault, or a defence against counter-attack). The French were also committed to the offensive, needing to expel the Germans from their territory, so it is no coincidence that they adopted a highly portable machine-rifle which could be carried and fired in the assault. The Germans, able to adopt a generally defensive posture on the Western Front from late 1914 to the spring of 1918, developed their machine gun techniques accordingly – with an emphasis on the provision of interlocking fire within many-layered defensive positions. On the mountainous Italian Front, both sides strove to develop the type of short-range, light automatic weapons best suited to the sort of sudden close combat that often resulted from the top-ography and weather conditions of their lofty battlefield. As Paddy Griffith has put it: 'The exclusive charmed circle which is conventionally drawn around the Great War's "tactical innovators" – whether Germans, ANZACs or tankies – turns out to be quite illusory, since tactical innovation was a game that almost everyone was playing, even including the woolly old cavalry generals them-selves.'[1]

It would be wrong however, to presume that such progressive thinking was applied on a comprehensive basis. As Colonel Hutchinson wrote with regard to the employment of machine guns: 'the persistence by some corps and divisional commanders in disregarding the lessons from previous experience remained marked; and, indeed, in some instances was continued until the Armistice'.[2] Naturally the British were not alone in this inability to adopt tactical advances universally – we should not forget the shamefully outmoded massed attacks carried out by some of the German infantry in 1918, or the cost in lives of the US Army's initial failure to apprehend the nature of battle on the Western Front. While tactical and technical instructions were promulgated in all armies, it would be dangerous to assume that they were followed without exception. All parties perceived a continuing need to reinforce good practice in their training manuals – even going to the lengths of disseminating 'Catechisms' of basic principles, intended to be learnt by rote. These efforts can only have been made because it was common knowledge that not all officers were applying the newly introduced tactics in the field.

Technological and economic limitations could provide further obstacles to the tide of wartime innovation. As noted previously, it is wrong to judge the weapons used by today's standards. The ability of armies to select and adopt new weapons was constrained by metallurgical considerations and manufacturing difficulties. Even before the war, armies did not always adopt the best weapons available to them (the Vickers gun being a notable exception). Their choice was circumscribed by tactical doctrines, patriotism and the need to ensure continuity of training, equipment and ammunition supply. The coming of war added another, overriding determinant: the extent to which each combatant's war economy would permit mass production or volume-purchases to be undertaken. Thus we see the Americans entering battle with a selection of French and British automatic weapons, despite having excellent indigenous designs; the Germans issuing a compromise light machine gun; the British opportunistically adopting the Lewis; the French reversing their pre-war distaste for the non-French Hotchkiss and their mass production of the unlovely CSRG. Less fortunate armies, such as those of Belgium, Italy, Russia, Turkey, Romania, Serbia and Bulgaria, were doomed to supplement inadequate (or non-existent) domestic production with machine guns purchased from their allies (who naturally prioritized their own armies' supply).

The tactical legacy

In the field of machine guns, as in many other aspects of military practice, the Great War set the tone for the decades to follow. In particular, the inter-war era and the Second World War saw automatic weapons employed largely in line with concepts developed between 1914 and 1918. The British and French continued to rely upon a platoon system in which light machine guns provided covering fire for the manoeuvres of riflemen and grenadiers – they simply upgraded their light automatics – replacing the CSRG with the Fusil-Mitrailleur M29/34 and the Lewis with the excellent Bren. The Americans retained faith in the BAR – possibly for too long – although its limitations were probably concealed by the fact that the large US platoon of the Second World War was armed with the self-loading M1 rifle.

Heavier machine guns were now firmly established as long-range weapons. In Britain this was officially recognized in 1936, when a process began of converting selected infantry battalions into machine gun battalions – thus partially reversing the decision to disband the MGC. Consequently, during the Second World War, just as in 1918, British Infantry Divisions incorporated a battalion of specialist machine-gunners. Their role was predominantly one of long-range support. To assist this task the paraphernalia of indirect fire, which had been developed on a semi-official basis during the First World War, was now officially procured and issued. This equipment ranged from upgraded versions of the slide rules and protractors, which MGC officers had formerly been obliged to purchase for themselves, to aiming lamps, artillery-like directors and plotters and, finally, the 'crowning touch' (as Dolf Goldsmith calls it) the Sight, Dial, MG. This was a more sophisticated version of the German indirect fire sight of 1918. It was graduated out to 4,400 yards. This astonishing range was facilitated by the introduction of the new Mk VIII cartridge, with a heavy 'boat-tailed' bullet specifically intended for use in the Vickers gun. During the latter stages of the war, this range was utilized to its full, when MG battalions participated in the firing of 'pepperpot' barrages, which involved the coordination of Vickers guns with every heavy weapon not involved in the divisional artillery plan. Thus the sectors of enemy territory would be deluged not only with machine gun fire but, simultaneously, with the fire of mortars, anti-tank guns and light and heavy anti-aircraft guns.

The nature of the work undertaken by the British MG battalions was emphasized by a change to their structure which occurred in 1943, when they were reorganized to incorporate a company of heavy 4.2-inch mortars, which boasted a similar range to the Vickers. This was also significant marker for the future, as, in subsequent years, the traditional support role of machine guns was increasingly usurped by heavier weapons. These include heavy machine guns (typically of .50-inch or 12.7mm calibre) and, in recent years, automatic 40mm grenade launchers (which have an effective range of around 1,200m). Principally however, it is the mortar which has taken over the role in which the machine gun reigned supreme from 1915 until 1945. Even relatively light mortars, such as the popular 81mm calibre, can equal the range of rifle-calibre machine gun fire. The mortar has also proved a major deterrent to any attempt to use 'medium machine guns' (as those of rifle-calibre became known) in a direct fire role. Vickers gunners during the Second World War were – if not dug in in barrage positions – obliged to use 'shoot and scoot' tactics: vacating their firing positions before the inevitable reprisal arrived in the form of a German mortar 'stonk'. The Vickers was, due to its innate qualities, able to defy technological progress – occasionally performing prodigies in the hills or Korea or Southern Arabia until the 1960s. It did not leave service with the British Army until 1968. By this time another iteration of the machine gun concept was standard issue in most armies (including Britain's): namely the General Purpose Machine Gun.

The technological legacy

The General Purpose Machine Gun (GPMG) originated in Germany at the height of the Great War. It was proposed that a 'universal' machine gun (*Einheitsmaschinengewehr*) might be developed to take the place of both the MG08 and MG08/15 – combining the most of the accuracy and sustained fire ability of the former with some of the portability of the latter. Experimental examples of what was known as the MG16 were produced, but the pressures of war production meant that only its tripod, the Dreifuss 16 saw service in the field, being manufactured concurrently with the Schlitten 08 during the latter part of the war. The MG16 was essentially a tripod-mounted MG08/15, with the butt and pistol grip replaced by a spade-grip and trigger unit at the rear. It was not until Germany's rearmament under the Nazis that the *Einheitsmasch-inengewehr* concept came to maturity in the form of the MG34 and, later, the MG42 – it was these weapons that were anachronistically nicknamed 'Spandaus' by the Western Allies, although, ironically, the mighty Spandau Arsenal had shrunk to nothing more than a munitions repair facility by the time of the Second World War. German platoon tactics reflected the lessons that they had taken from the First World War – with the machine gun in its LMG configuration providing the firepower, and the riflemen acting as its auxiliaries. Meanwhile, with the addition of its tripod and ranging and sighting equipment, the same gun was used by the battalion machine gun company in an indirect role.[3] Germany's opponents were greatly impressed by the volume of fire delivered by the MG34 and MG42. Probably more so than the users of these weapons, who were obliged to lug huge quantities of ammunition around – particularly for the MG42, which had a cyclic rate of 1,200 rounds per minute (double that of a Vickers gun). Most armies during the immediate post-war period therefore investigated the possibility of manufacturing or purchasing GPMGs. By the latter part of the 1960s, all major armies were equipped with them. For example, Britain issued a version of the widely distributed Belgian-designed FN MAG, the USA employed the M60, and the Soviet

Union had introduced the PK. Several armies, including that of the Federal Republic of Germany, relied upon upgraded versions of the MG42.

Another invention of the First World War which did not flourish until later was the submachine-gun (SMG). The word 'submachine-gun', which has since achieved almost universal usage in the English-speaking world, was coined in the USA to describe the weapon conceived by General John T Thompson. Thompson had originally intended his gun as a 'Trench Broom', but the war ended before development was complete. Thereafter the Thompson pursued a chequered career in the hands of IRA men, strike-breakers, Federal Agents and, ultimately, Allied troops during the Second World War. It also acquired its own considerable cachet as an item of material culture – a process well described by John Ellis.[4] In terms of military use, it is not surprising that the earliest enthusiasts for this class of weapon were those who had pioneered its development – the Italians and the Germans. Other countries needed to experience their effectiveness at first hand before feeling it necessary to issue them to their own troops. Ironically it was two of these latecomers who were to take the SMG concept to its extreme. Britain's wartime economy spawned the Sten – perhaps the most brutally functional expression of the submachine-gun (or machine carbine as it was called in Britain at the time). Meanwhile the Soviet Union had been persuaded of the potency of the submachine-gun by the bloody nose that their troops had received at the hands of the Finns during the 1939–40 'Winter War'. The Finns had made effective use of their indigenous Suomi SMG. When Germany invaded the USSR, simple SMGs were seen as an ideal weapon for mass production by Soviet arsenals: and they were indeed produced in extraordinary quantities. The Red Amy became unique in equipping whole units – up to battalion size – entirely with submachine-guns.[5]

However, even as the SMG reached its apogee as a military weapon, new developments were making it obsolete. For it was the Second World War which witnessed the first volume production of the assault rifle – the weapon foreshadowed by Fedorov's *Avtomat* of 1916. The basis of all assault rifle design was the use of a cartridge intermediate between the short-range pistol ammunition used by SMGs and the overly powerful rifle cartridges bequeathed by the tactical thinking of the late nineteenth century. Analysis of infantry firefights in the Great War, particularly by the Germans, indicated that virtually all occurred at ranges of less than 400 metres. Despite this, all armies during the inter-war era remained wedded to their pre-1914 rifle ammunition – not least because money was short and huge stocks of it were still available. The return of war provided an impetus for change and it was the Germans who led the way, issuing an effective assault rifle, the MP43, to its troops during 1944. Fortunately for the Allied cause, Germany's war industry proved unable to manufacture enough of this weapon (subsequently renamed MP44 and – at Hitler's behest – *Sturmgewehr* 44) to supplant the bolt-action rifle in service. The Red Army soon became aware of the new weapon, and swiftly began development of its own intermediate cartridge. In 1948, they introduced AK47 – the brainchild of Mikhail Timofeovich Kalashnikov; a weapon which has become a modern icon in its own right: primarily as a symbol of armed revolutionary struggle. Both the Germans and the Soviets used cartridges of the same calibre as their standard rifle ammunition, but shortened. A subsequent wave of development led to the general adoption of a new generation of small-calibre, high-velocity cartridges, such as the NATO 5.56mm round and the Russian 5.45 × 39mm. These cartridges are optimized for use at ranges out to around half a kilometre and, despite their small size, their bullets are unpleasantly effective at causing wounds, largely due to their inherent instability.[6] The issue of the assault rifle to infantry units has been complemented by the adoption of 'Light Support Weapons' (LSWs) or 'Squad Automatic Weapons' (SAWs) in the same calibre. While the LSW/SAW enhances the firepower of small units, no weapon chambered for cartridges with such a limited effective range can carry out the traditional support role of machine guns. Consequently machine guns have been further marginalized. The GPMG concept has effectively been killed off (for a SAW and an MG now need to chamber different types of cartridge), and support is more than ever provided by mortars, grenade launchers and heavy machine guns (although properly mounted GPMGs are still capable of indirect fire – in what the British Army calls 'map predicted mode'). Meanwhile, submachine-guns have lost their battlefield role, although they have enjoyed something of a renaissance in recent years as the weapon of choice for specialized anti-terrorist formations. Thus, it was the general adoption of intermediate cartridges – themselves a product of lessons learned between 1914 and 1918 – that ended the influence of the Great War on infantry fire tactics. At least, this remained the case until the second decade of the 21st century, when full-bore ammunition once again found a role in the context of long-range engagements in Afghanistan.

The machine gun myth

Previous chapters have revealed the surprisingly positive popular image enjoyed by the machine gun – even in the face of the unprecedented destruction of human life that resulted from the industrialized warfare of which it formed a key element. A further layer of favourable symbolism was added by machine guns captured from the enemy. It was a consequence of the rising importance of machine guns on the battlefields of the Great War that their capture came to be seen as a measure of the success of any offensive operation. In former wars, such significance had adhered only to artillery pieces. Now the number of captured machine guns was recorded after each attack. As a con-comitant of this development, machine guns very naturally became sought after as trophies of war. After a successful action in April 1917, Captain Graham Greenwell wrote that 'Our captured [machine] guns are fine trophies, and I have already had them stamped "Captured by 'B' Company 1/4 Oxford and Bucks Lt. Infty." They will go to Oxford at the end of the war.'[7] In the following year, *The Times* extolled the use of such trophies in raising war-funds, suggesting that: 'A captured gun, grimed with the mud of France or Flanders, a heavy minenwerfer that perhaps a month ago was shelling a British first line trench, a machine gun that may have "held-up" half a battalion till its team were bayonetted [sic] by the vanguard of our advancing infantry, make an even more effectual appeal.'[8]

After the Armistice, a more ordered system of trophy distribution was put in place by the Army Council, which set up a

> Departmental Committee to deal with all the questions relating thereto, and to watch the interests of the Imperial War Museum in consultation with the museum committee. The normal procedure is for guns and other trophies sent to this country from France and other theatres of war, to be claimed as having been captured by certain units. If the claims of these units are substantiated the com-manding officers are given the opportunity of determining whether the trophies should be presented to the Regimental Depot, the Imperial War Museum, or some City, Borough, etc.[9]

So, captured German machine guns embarked on new post-war lives as emblems of victory in regimental headquarters, or proudly displayed by municipal authorities at town halls, or in museums. No less than 4,000 cap-tured machine guns were sent to Canada.[10] So many remained in Australia in 1942 that they were gathered up and rechambered for .303-inch ammunition, in expectation of an imminent Japanese invasion. The numbers involved are indicated by the fact that 1,500 of these modified guns were created – even after many were 'cannibalized' to provide parts for others.[11]

Aside from its fetishization as a trophy, the machine gun might be said to have achieved its apotheosis (in Britain at least) in 1925, when real Vickers guns were dipped in bronze to adorn the plinth of the Machine Gun Corps Memorial. There is a mystery, then, in the process by which the machine gun gained the iconic significance it has today as a symbol of the 'futile' slaughter of the Western Front and, it might be said, as a cipher for the First World War as a whole. I would suggest that the roots of the machine gun's modern-day popular image lie largely in the haphazard development of the historiography of the Great War.

The numerous memoirs and first-hand accounts of the war, which appeared in its wake, do not tend to elevate the machine gun to any position of dominance among other aspects or, indeed, other weapon systems of the war (unless, of course they were written by machine-gunners). However, those at some remove from actual combat were quick to seize upon the machine gun as a symbol of both the carnage and the 'stalemate' of the Western Front. I would suggest that this was due to the fact that the ostensibly simple 'point and shoot' cause and effect of machine gun fire, as popularly conceived, offered a straightforward way of explaining it. Thus, as early as 1927 we find none other than Winston Churchill in his book *The World Crisis* writing: 'If only the generals had not been content to fight machine-gun bullets with the breasts of gallant men, and think that was waging war'. This was both a first-class example of the great man's ability to coin a ringing phrase and of his willingness to substitute such persuasive eloquence for hard fact when writing his historical works. It was not long before this undue emphasis of the machine gun was taken up by other influential figures.

The military theorist and commentator Captain Basil Liddell Hart was, perhaps, the foremost of these. Liddell Hart had served in the war, but appears not to have suffered unduly from machine gun fire during his brief time in action. Indeed, he confessed to fearing shells and aerial bombs far more than bullets.[12] He was in reserve when his battalion went into action on the first day of the Somme but, shortly afterwards, was invalided home after becoming a victim of an early use of phosgene gas shells at Mametz Wood. He subsequently established himself as the most renowned military thinker of his day and, as military correspondent for the *Daily Telegraph* and (later) *The Times*, his influence extended beyond merely military circles. Hart's adoption of radical (often idiosyncratic) tactical theories drove him to take issue with most aspects of British First World War strategy and tactics. At an early stage he became a proponent of armoured warfare, and this appears to have led him to exaggerate the importance of machine gun fire – it being the threat that the tank was designed to neutralize. His identification of the machine gun as the dominant weapon of the war was therefore of post-war origin; but it became a central tenet of his beliefs. By 1933 he was able to state with confidence in a lecture to a military audience that: 'The one man who bestrode the World War like a Colossus was Hiram Maxim. Generals and statesmen became helpless puppets in the grip of his machine gun. The machine gun was, and still is, the dominant fact in land warfare.'[13] The variation of this statement which is reproduced at the head of this chapter was published in the same year in his book: *The Future of Infantry*.

Energetic and self-promoting, Liddell Hart did not limit himself to propagating his views merely in his own work. His network of contacts – many of whom were pleased to receive his advice – was considerable. Among them was the wartime Prime Minister David Lloyd George. Hart acted as military adviser for the latter's *War Memoirs*, wherein the machine gun was characterized as 'The most lethal weapon of the war'. As we have seen, Lloyd George was eager to puff his own achievements in increasing machine gun production whilst Minister of Munitions, while simultaneously defaming his old enemies in the wartime High Command. Therefore it was in his interest to portray the weapon as being of supreme importance. The former premier's book was hugely successful and influential. Indeed, the deliberately misleading section dealing with the procurement of machine guns has continued to be quoted, without qualification, in books right up to the present day.

The influence of Lloyd George and Liddell Hart was certainly apparent twenty years later, when a new wave of popular histories of the Great War began to appear. Following a period when the immediacy of the Second World War had eclipsed interest in the First, these books simultaneously fed upon and fostered a renewed public interest in the conflict. Due to the fifty-year rule on the release of official papers then in place, the authors of these works had, of necessity, to rely upon the secondary sources already available. Thus the erroneous placement of the machine gun at the heart of the tactical conundrum that was the Western Front was, to some extent, simply a function of repetition. Widely credited with the being the first of this new wave of Great War histories, *In Flanders Fields*, by Leon Wolff, quotes 'Boney' Fuller when he writes of hapless British soldiery pitted against 'thousands of armoured machine-guns (that new and utterly frustrating "concentrated essence of infantry")'.[14] In another early example of this new wave of First World War books, Alan Clark was moved to envision (evidently in ignorance of the approved way to fire a machine gun) 'that most haunting of all the sounds of trench warfare – the drawn-out rattle of a long burst on the machine-gun'.[15] Clark was of course the protégé of Liddell Hart. Another of the latter's correspondents, A J P Taylor, was clear:

> One man with a machine gun, protected by mounds of earth, was more powerful than advancing masses ... The machine gun completed the contrast between the speed with which men could arrive at the battlefield by rail, and the slowness with which they moved when they were there. Indeed they did not move at all. The opposing lines

congealed, grew solid. The generals on both sides stared at these lines impotently and without understanding. They went on staring for nearly four years.[16]

This conception was undoubtedly reinforced by popular representations of the war. The wartime press had abounded with illustrations of British heroes gamely taking on emplaced German machine guns and putting their shaven-headed crews to the bayonet. The officially sanctioned film *The Battle of the Somme* (1916) must also have exerted a significant effect, as it is estimated that it was viewed by an astonishing twenty million people when first released.[17] It contains a scene purporting to show troops going 'over the top' on 1 July 1916. Four of them fall as they advance – apparent victims of machine gun fire. It is now considered that this iconic sequence – 'a classic part of the imagery of the First World War' – was faked at a trench mortar school, well behind the lines.[18] Furthermore, subsequent film and television productions might well have reinforced this picture, for the simple reason that it is certainly easier and cheaper to recreate machine gun fire for such purposes than it is to replicate an artillery barrage. Incidentally the cinema of the post-1945 era has established a parallel iconography for the machine gun as a symbol of the modern age. It appears in more than one Western as a metaphor for the march of 'progress' bringing an end to the romantic era of the Old West – a curious inversion of the Futurist's enthusiastic identification of the machine gun as a harbinger of the machine age.

By the time the new thirty-year rule on the release of papers was introduced in the Public Records Act of 1967, the image was evidently firmly established outside the historical community. Paul Fussell, in his celebrated literary study *The Great War and Modern Memory*, lambasted the poet David Jones's attempt to position the Western Front in the context of human experiences of war reaching back to ancient times, with the words: 'The war will not be understood in traditional terms: the machine gun alone makes it so special and unexampled that it simply can't be talked about as if it were one of the conventional wars of history.'[19] The repetition of an easily grasped theme eventually established a new orthodoxy. Dan Todman, in his excellent study of public perceptions of the Great War, quotes the *Daily Telegraph* (in 1986) making a reference to 'ranks of brave men ordered forward through barbed wire and quagmire to throw themselves fruitlessly at fortified machine-gun positions'.[19] In this quote we see all the elements of the modern popular conception of the First World War – mud, incompetent (usually British) generals, wire, and – as the dynamic element – machine guns. As recently as 1993 Lyn Macdonald echoed the words of Liddell Hart and Taylor when she reiterated the machine gun-oriented view of the origins of trench warfare in the following paragraph:

> The Germans were outnumbered in places by as many as three to one but, thanks to machine-guns liberally sited along their trenches, they could repel attack after attack. Not for nothing was the machine-gun called the Queen of the Battlefield. Soon they would be calling it the Grim Reaper.[20]

Thus the machine gun has acquired an altogether darker image since the 1960s than it was ever burdened with while the Great War still raged. Now it is not uncommon to anthropomorphize the weapon as 'The Widow Maker' or the 'Grim Reaper'. In these guises it presides over a hellish vision of the First World War as a barbed wire-bound morass, lit by the eerie glare of parachute-flares, seeded with corpses and populated by rats 'as big as cats'. It 'scythes' down men in 'swathes' – presenting the generals with bloated 'butcher's bills' (this last linguistic reduction of men to meat appearing even in some serious works of history). Despite the testimony of history, art and literature to the fact that *all* wars have their horrors, this *Grand Guignol* treatment is almost exclusively reserved for the First World War – and the machine gun lies very near its heart.

So, ironically, although the tactical and technological legacy of machine guns in the Great War was an important factor in the conduct of war during the twentieth century, it has actually been outlived by the weapon's role as an icon of that conflict. Other automatic firearms developed in the wake of First World War technological advances have themselves enjoyed vogues as icons of material culture – the 'Tommy gun' in the hands of movie gangsters; the Kalashnikov assault rifle as the symbol of anti-imperialist struggle, or even – in recent years – the dubious chic of compact submachine-guns in the hands of the better equipped sort of drug dealer. However, it is hard to imagine any of these weapons attaining the enduring emblematic resonance that is enjoyed by the belt-fed, water-cooled machine gun devised by Hiram Maxim.

Notes

Prologue

1. C Duffy, *Through German Eyes* (2006), 168.
2. J Terraine, *General Jack's Diary* (2003), 145–6.
3. P Hart, *The Somme* (2005), 169.
4. Terraine, *Jack*, 146.
5. Duffy, *Through German Eyes*, 166.
6. Ibid., 165.
7. B Bond, *The First World War* (1991), p. vii.
8. See Bond, *First World War, The Unquiet Western Front* (2002); S Winter, *The Great War in History* (2005); Todman, *The Great War* (2005).
9. G Noon, 'Treatment of Casualties', in P Griffith (ed.), *British Fighting Methods in the Great War* (1996), 101–2.
10. J Terraine, *The Smoke and the Fire* (1981), 132.
11. Quoted in R Holmes, *Firing Line* (1994), 223.
12. See Todman, *Great War*.
13. S Audoin-Rouzeau and A Becker, *1914–1918* (2002), 19.

Chapter 1

1. D Goldsmith, *The Devil's Paintbrush* (1989), 333.
2. J Huon, *Proud Promise* (1995), 4–6.
3. I Hogg, *The Complete Machine-Gun* (1979), 18.
4. G Hutchinson, *Machine Guns* (2004), 63.
5. Ibid., 64.
6. H Maxim, *My Life* (1915), 197.
7. See D Goldsmith, *The Browning Machine Gun*, vol. 1 (2005).
8. Ibid., 9–11.
9. Bruce Williams Papers.
10. A Edwards, *British Secondary Small Arms, 1914–1919*, pt 3 (2008), 82.
11. The gun is preserved in the Imperial War Museum.
12. Hutchinson, *Machine Guns*, 88.
13. Ibid., 92.
14. D Herrmann, *The Arming of Europe and the Making of the First World War* (1996), 66.
15. Wade, 'From Maxim to Vickers', *Army Quarterly*, 28 (1934), 114–15.

16. Herrmann, *Arming of Europe*, 70.
17. A Allfrey, *Man of Arms* (1989), 61.
18. E Brose, *The Kaiser's Army* (2001), 143, 175.
19. I take these figures from Brose, *Kaiser's Army*, 227, and Goldsmith, *Devil's Paintbrush*, 158–60. The latter reproduces a German document concerning the provision of armoured shields for all MGs in German service in August 1914. This document should be treated with care, as it seems evident that spare shields were also issued – e.g. MG Companies (which we know to have had six guns each, if at full establishment) received ten shields.
20. *Les Mitrailleuses*.
21. Ibid.
22. D A Armstrong, *Bullets and Bureaucrats* (1982), 158, 175.
23. Bruce Williams Papers.
24. Wade, 'From Maxim to Vickers', 115.

Chapter 2
1. M Walsh, *CRW Nevinson* (2002), 146.
2. Gough, 'A Terrible Beauty' (in prep.).
3. Marinetti, 140.
4. N N Golovine, *The Russian Army in the World War* (1993), 130–1.
5. See J Schindler, *Isonzo* (2001).
6. D Showalter, *Tannenberg* (1991), 239.
7. Brose, *Kaiser's Army*, 204.
8. H Strachan, *The First World War*, vol. 1 (2001), 237.
9. H D Handrich, *Sturmgewehr* (2004), 5.
10. A Clayton, *Paths of Glory* (2003), 207.
11. Wade, 'From Maxim to Vickers', 118.
12. B Bairnsfather, *Bullets and Billets* (1916), 294.
13. Cornish, 'Unlawful Wounding' (2014).
14. J House, *Toward Combined Arms Warfare* (1950), 13.
15. Showalter, *Tannenberg*, 184.
16. H Colin, *La Division de Fer* (1930), 27.
17. In 1915–16 921 of these small units were formed. See H Cron, *Imperial German Army* (2002), 121–2.
18. G Wynne, *If Germany Attacks* (1940), 77.
19. Ibid., 76.
20. D Goldsmith, *The Grand Old Lady of No Man's Land* (1994), 22.
21. National Archive MUN 4/2738.

22. *Les Mitrailleuses.*
23. Ibid.
24. T Travers, *The Killing Ground* (1987), 66.
25. Wade, 'From Maxim to Vickers', 118.
26. R Wright, 'Machine Gun Tactics and Organization', *Army Quarterly*, 1 (1921), 291.
27. Hutchinson, *Machine Guns*, 132 (the author misspells the officer's name as 'Ludwick').
28. Ibid., 141–2.
29. SS109.

Chapter 3

1. D Lloyd George, *War Memoirs*, vol. 2 (1933), 612–13.
2. Wright, 'Machine Gun Tactics', 292.
3. P Griffith, *Battle Tactics of the Western Front* (1994), 128.
4. A Russell, *With the MGC from Grantham to Cologne* (1923), 15.
5. Machine Gun Notes, lecture notes.
6. *US Machine Gun Notes No. 2*, 28.
7. J H Luxford, *With the Machine Gunners in France and Palestine* (1923), 34.
8. H Davis, 'The Employment of Machine Guns with a Battalion of Infantry', *Journal of the Royal United Services Institution*, 67/468 (1922), 695.
9. Goldsmith, *Grand Old Lady*, 150.
10. F von Merkatz, *New Methods of Machine Gun Fire* (1916), 42.
11. P Chasseaud, *Artillery's Astrologers* (1999), 90–1.
12. SS106 (Amendments May 1917).
13. E Jünger, *Storm of Steel* (2004), 78.
14. Duffy, *Through German Eyes*, 276.
15. A Taylor, *The First World War* (1978), 139–40.
16. G Coppard, *With a Machine Gun to Cambrai* (1969), 89–91.
17. B Rawling, *Surviving Trench Warfare* (1992), 37–8.
18. Hutchinson, *Machine Guns*, 186–7.
19. Russell, *With the MGC*, 60.
20. Wright, 'Machine Gun Tactics', 306–7.
21. Horne papers.
22. SS487.
23. Cron, *Imperial German Army*, 122.
24. *US Machine Gun Notes No. 2*, 14.
25. C Crutchley, *Machine Gunners* (1973), 39.

26. See Audoin-Rouzeau and Becker, *1914–1918* and J Ramsden, *Don't Mention the War* (2007).

27. D Hibberd, *Wilfred Owen* (2002), 349–50.

Chapter 4

1. W Easterly, *The Belgian Rattlesnake* (1998), 82.
2. *Lewis Gun Mechanism Made Easy*, 21–2.
3. Quoted in Griffith, *Battle Tactics*, 130.
4. SS197, 31.
5. NA MUN 4/2738.
6. J Lee, 'Some Lessons of the Somme', in B Bond (ed.), *Look to Your Front* (1999), 81–4.
7. SS197.
8. See Huon, *Proud Promise*.
9. G Demaison and Y Buffetaut, *Honour Bound* (1995), 21.
10. *Manual of the Chief of Platoon*, 81.
11. Ibid., 28. This organization is not stipulated in the previous year's edn of this manual.
12. See Demaison and Buffetaut, *Honour Bound*, 93–4, and *La Mitrailleuse*.
13. J Buchan, *The Battle of the Somme* (n.d.), 31.
14. See Edwards, *British Secondary Small Arms*, 81–9.
15. Davis, 'Employment', 695.
16. Duffy, *Through German Eyes*, 279.
17. SS486.
18. SS579.
19. Goldsmith, *Devil's Paintbrush*, 170.
20. E Ludendorff, *My War Memories*, vol. 1 (n.d.), 338.
21. SS579, SS486, SS487, SS544.
22. H Cron, *Infanterie Regiment Nr 60* (1926), 314.
23. L Wolff, *Das Königlich Sächsische Infanterie Regiment 'Kronprinz' Nr 104* (1926–8), vol. 3, p. 12.
24. Allan, 'The Bergmann LMG15 Series'.
25. SS667.
26. See http://world.guns.ru/assault/as86-e.htm
27. D N Bolotin, *Soviet Small Arms and Ammunition* (1995), 125–6.
28. Demaison and Buffetaut, *Honour Bound*, 155–6.
29. I have used the term submachine-gun (originally coined in the USA) throughout as it is now the commonly accepted term for such weapons, rather than Machine-Pistol, Machine-Carbine, etc.

30. V Bobba, 'Pistola mitragliatrice Villar-Perosa mod. 1915', *Quaderni di Oplogia* 11 (2000), 71.
31. See L Sengewitz, 'Steyr-Armeepistole M12/P16', *Deutsche Waffen-Journal*, 6 (June 1980).
32. It should be noted that Christian Örtner gives a contrasting summary of events, in which Major Fuchs is not mentioned. See Örtner, *Storm Troops* (2005), 230.

Chapter 5
1. R Doughty, *Pyrrhic Victory* (2005), 350–1.
2. *Machine Gun Notes No. 2*, 33.
3. WO 158/418.
4. *Machine Gun Notes No. 2*, 33.
5. Luxford, *With the Machine Gunners*, 71.
6. *Machine Gun Notes No. 1*, 203.
7. Horne Papers.
8. Störz, *Rifle and Carbine 98* (2006), 329–30.
9. SS703.
10. See Wolff, *Das Königlich Sächsische Infanterie Regiment*, vol. 3, pp. 8–9.
11. WO 158/332, Conclusion.
12. Illustrated in Goldsmith, *Devil's Paintbrush*, 183–5.
13. Wolff, *Das Königlich Sächsische Infanterie Regiment*, vol. 3, p. 9.
14. F Myrvang, *MG34–MG42 German Universal Machineguns* (2002), 337–48.
15. A Russell, *The Machine Gunner* (1977), 119.
16. Quoted in N Steel and P Hart, *Passchendaele: The Sacrificial Ground* (2000), 291.
17. Horne papers.
18. WO 95/275.
19. WO 95/1193.
20. Hutchinson, *History and Memoirs ...* (1919), 35.
21. Machine Gun Notes.
22. G Sheffield, *Forgotten Victory* (2002), 253.
23. M Grotelueschen, *The AEF Way of War* (2007), 59.

Chapter 6
1. T Travers, 'The Evolution of British Strategy and Tactics on the Western Front in 1918', *Journal of Modern History*, 54/2 (1990), 187.
2. WO158/332 (Conclusion).
3. Machine Gun Notes.

4. Crutchley, *Machine Gunner*, 101.
5. Wolff, *Das Königlich Sächsische Infanterie Regiment*, vol. 2, pp. 481–7.
6. H D Götz, *Die Deutschen Militärgewehre und Maschinenpistolen* (1981), 1561.
7. Wolff, *Das Königlich Sächsische Infanterie Regiment*, vol. 3, p. 25.
8. Horne Papers.
9. J Coop, *The Story of the 55th (West Lancashire) Division* (1919), 137.
10. Mallett thesis: see 'Web sources' section of Bibliography.
11. S Schreiber, *Shock Army of the British Empire* (1997), 104.
12. T Nenninger, 'Tactical Dysfunction in the AEF', *Military Affairs*, 51/4 (1987), 178.
13. Grotelueschen, *AEF Way*, 148.
14. Ibid., 348.
15. S Bull, *German Assault Troops of the First World War* (2007), 129.
16. Grotelueschen, *AEF Way*, 103.
17. H D Handrich, *Sturmgewehr* (2004), 5.
18. Örtner, 'Die K.u.K. Sturmtruppe 1916–1918', in *Österreichische Militärgeschicte*, vol. 6 (1998), 211.
19. Von Merkatz, *New Methods*, 14.
20. B Rawling, *Surviving Trench Warfare* (1992), 213–14.
21. Schrieber, *Shock Army*, 123–5.
22. A van Walleghem, *De oorlog te Dickebusch* (1967), 57.

Epilogue

1. Griffith, *Battle Tactics*, 193.
2. Hutchinson, *Machine Guns*, 179.
3. Myrwang, *MG34–MG42*, 335–55.
4. J Ellis, *The Social History of the Machine Gun* (1987), 149–63.
5. Cornish, 'Pistolet Pulomet', *Military Illustrated*, 82 (1985), 37.
6. Cornish, 'Unlawful Wounding' (in prep.).
7. G Greenwell, *An Infant in Arms* (1972), 175.
8. *The Times* (6 June 1918).
9. NA T1/12438.
10. Vance, 'Tangible Demonstrations of a Great Victory', *Material History Review*, 42 (1995), 50.
11. Skennerton, *Australian Service Machineguns* (1989), 54–7.
12. Danchev, *Alchemist of War* (1998), 50–1.
13. B Liddell Hart, 'An International Force', *International Affairs*, 12/2 (1933), 213.
14. L Wolff, *In Flanders Fields* (1959), 5.

15. A Clark, *The Donkeys* (1961), 65.
16. Taylor, *First World War*, 34.
17. Todman, *Great War*, 15.
18. R. Smither, 'A Wonderful Idea of Fighting', *Imperial War Museum Review*, 3 (1988), 4–6.
19. P. Fussell, *The Great War and Modern Memory* (1975), 153.
20. Todman, *Great War*, 38.
21. L Macdonald, *The Death of Innocence* (1993), 9.

Bibliography

Unpublished Sources
Imperial War Museum, Dept of Documents:
  Bruce-Williams Papers.
  Papers of General Lord Horne, File 57.
Imperial War Museum, Dept of Printed Books:
  Machine Gun Corps Training Centre Staff Notes.
  Machine Gun Notes (From Grantham Training Course).
National Archive MUN 4/2738:
  WO 158/332
  WO 158/418
  WO 95/1193
  WO 95/275
  Allan, D. 'The Bergmann LMG15 Series' (unpublished paper, 1999).

Published training manuals and pamphlets
SS106. *Notes on the Tactical Employment of Machine Guns and Lewis Guns* (March 1916).
SS122. *Some Notes on Lewis Guns and Machine Guns* (Sept. 1916).
SS155. *Notes on dealing with Hostile machine guns in an advance* (April 1917).
SS192. *The Employment of Machine Guns: Part 1 Tactical* (Jan. 1918).
SS201. *Tactical Summary of MG Operations*, 1 (Oct. 1917).
SS197. *The Tactical Employment of Lewis Guns* (Jan. 1918).
SS486. *Extracts from German Documents Dealing With 'Lessons Drawn from the Battle of the Somme'.*
SS487. *Order of the 6th Bavarian Division Regarding Machine Guns, 3 September 1916.*
SS544. *Experience of the Recent Fighting at Verdun.*
SS553a. *Experience of the German 1st Army in the Somme Battle.*
SS579. *Extracts from the Experiences of the Sixth German Army in the Employment of the '08/'15 Light Machine Gun* (June 1917).
SS667. *Provisional Instruction for Light Machine-Gun Platoons. Translation of a captured Austrian Document* (1917).
General Staff. *Handbook of the German Army 1914* (London: IWM, 2002).
— *Handbook of the Italian Army 1913* (London: IWM, 1995).

Lewis Gun Mechanism Made Easy (London: Gale & Polden, various edns).
The Machine Gun Corps Magazine (Nov. 1916–Dec. 1918).
Machine Gun Notes No. 1, May 1917 (Washington, DC: Government Printing Office, 1917).
Machine Gun Notes No. 2, February 1918 (Washington, DC: Government Printing Office, 1918).
Manual of the Chief of Platoon of Infantry, translated from the French edn of Jan. 1917 (HQ American Expeditionary Force, 1917).
Manuel du Chef de Section d'Infanterie (GQG, 1916).
Merkatz, F von. *New Methods of Machine Gun Fire* (Washington, DC: The United States Infantry Association, 1916).
Mitrailleuses françaises d'Infanterie: Guide de l'Elève-Mitrailleur (Écoles d'Infanterie, 1918).
Notes on the use of Machine Guns in Trench Warfare (Washington, DC: Government Printing Office, 1917).
War Office. *Textbook of Small Arms* (London: HMSO, 1929).

Secondary Sources
Allfrey, A. *Man of Arms: The Life and Legend of Sir Basil Zaharoff* (London: Weidenfeld & Nicolson, 1989).
Armstrong, David A. *Bullets and Bureaucrats: The Machine Gun and the United States Army, 1861–1916* (Westport, CT: Greenwood Press, 1982).
Audoin-Rouzeau, S and Becker, A. *1914–1918: Understanding the Great War* (London: Profile Books, 2002).
Bairnsfather, B. *Bullets and Billets* (London: Grant Richards, 1916).
Baker-Carr, C. *From Chauffeur to Brigadier* (London: Ernest Benn Ltd, 1930).
Ballou, J. *Rock in a Hard Place: The Browning Automatic Rifle* (Cobourg: Collector Grade Publications, 2000).
Bidwell, S and Graham, D. *Fire Power* (London: Allen & Unwin, 1982).
Bobba, V. 'Pistola mitragliatrice Villar-Perosa mod. 1915', *Quaderni di Oplogia* 11/2nd Semester (Circulo Culturale Armigeri de Piave, 2000).
Bolotin, D N. *Soviet Small-Arms and Ammunition* (Hyvinkää: Finnish Arms Museum Foundation, 1995).
Bond, B. *Liddell Hart: A Study of his Military Thought* (London: Cassell, 1977).
— *The First World War and British Military History* (Oxford: Clarendon Press 1991).
— *The Unquiet Western Front* (Cambridge: CUP, 2002).
Brose, E. *The Kaiser's Army* (Oxford: OUP, 2001).
Buchan, J. *The Battle of the Somme: First Phase* (London: Nelson, n.d.).

Bull, S. *German Assault Troops of the First World War* (Stroud: Spellmount, 2007).

Chappell, M. *The Vickers Machine Gun* (Okehampton: Wessex Military Publishing, 1989).

Chasseaud, P. *Artillery's Astrologers* (Lewes: Mapbooks, 1999).

Clark, A. *The Donkeys* (London: Hutchinson, 1961).

Clayton, A. *Paths of Glory: The French Army 1914–18* (London: Cassell, 2003).

Colin, H. *La Division de Fer 1914–1918* (Paris: Payot, 1930).

Coop, J. *The Story of the 55th (West Lancashire) Division* (Liverpool: Liverpool Daily Post, 1919).

Coppard, G. *With a Machine Gun to Cambrai* (London: HMSO, 1969).

Cornish, P. 'Pistolet Pulomet', *Military Illustrated*, 82 (March 1995).

— '"Just a Boyish Habit" ...? British and Commonwealth War Trophies in the First World War', in P Cornish and N J Saunders (eds), *Contested Objects* (London: Routledge, 2009).

— 'Unlawful Wounding: Projectiles, Politics and Propaganda', in P Cornish and N J Saunders (eds), *Bodies in Conflict: Corporeality, Materiality, and Transformation* (London: Routledge, 2014).

Cron, H. *Imperial German Army 1914–18* (Solihull: Ilion, 2002).

— *Infanterie Regiment Markgraf Karl Nr 60 In dem Grosse Kriege 1914–1918* (Berlin: Schmidt, 1926).

Crutchley, C. *Machine Gunner 1914–18* (Northampton: Crutchley, 1973).

Danchev, A. *Alchemist of War: The Life of Basil Liddell Hart* (London: Weidenfeld & Nicholson, 1998).

Davis, H. 'The Employment of Machine Guns with a Battalion of Infantry: With Special Reference to the Indian Frontier', *Journal of the Royal United Services Institution*, 67/468 (1922).

Demaison, G and Buffetaut, Y. *Honour Bound: The Chauchat Machine Rifle* (Cobourg: Collector Grade Publications, 1995).

Doughty, R. *Pyrrhic Victory* (Cambridge: Belknap, 2005).

Duffy, C. *Through German Eyes: The British and the Somme 1916* (London: Weidenfeld & Nicolson, 2006).

Dunn, J. *The War the Infantry Knew* (London: Cardinal, 1989).

Easterly, W. *The Belgian Rattlesnake* (Cobourg: Collector Grade Publications, 1998).

Eberle, M. *World War 1 and the Weimar Artists* (New Haven: Yale University Press, 1985).

Edwards, A. *British Secondary Small Arms 1914–1919*, part 3, *Land Service Small Arms* (Canterbury: Solo Publications, 2008).

Ellis, J. *The Social History of the Machine Gun* (London: Cresset, 1987).

Ezell, E. *Kalashnikov: The Arms and the Man* (Cobourg: Collector Grade Publications, 2001).

Flint, R (ed.). *Marinetti: Selected Writings* (London: Secker & Warburg, 1972).

Fussell, P. *The Great War and Modern Memory* (New York: OUP, 1975).

Gabriel, E. *Die Hand-und Faustfeuerwaffen der Hapsburgischen Heere* (Vienna: Österreichischer Bundesverlag, 1990).

Goldsmith, D. *The Devil's Paintbrush* (Cobourg: Collector Grade Publications, 1989).

— *The Grand Old Lady of No Man's Land* (Cobourg: Collector Grade Publications, 1994).

— *The Browning Machine Gun*, vol. 1 (Cobourg: Collector Grade Publications, 2005).

Golovine, N N. *The Russian Army in the World War* (New Haven, CT: Yale University Press, 1931).

Gooch, J. 'Italy during the First World War', in A Millet and W Murray (eds) *Military Effectiveness*, vol. 1 (Boston: Allen & Unwin, 1988).

Görtz, J. 'Weiso Maschinenpistole "18.I"', *Deutsche Waffen-Journal*, 12 (Dec. 1983).

Götz, H-D. *Die Deutschen Militärgewehre und Maschinenpistolen 1871–1945* (Stuttgart: Motorbuch Verlag, 1981).

Gough, P. *'A Terrible Beauty': War, Art and the Imagination, 1914–1919* (in preparation).

Grafton, C. *The Canadian 'Emma Gees'* (London, Ontario: Canadian Machine Gun Corps Assoc., 1938).

Greenwell, G. *An Infant in Arms* (London: Allen Lane, 1972).

Griffith, P. *Battle Tactics of the Western Front* (New Haven, CT: Yale University Press, 1994).

Grotelueschen, M. *The AEF Way of War* (New York: Cambridge University Press, 2007).

Handrich, H-D. *Sturmgewehr* (Coburg Ontario: Collector Grade, 2004).

Hart, P. *The Somme* (London: Weidenfeld & Nicolson, 2005).

Hawkey, A. *The Amazing Hiram Maxim* (Staplehurst: Spellmount, 2001).

Herrmann, D. *The Arming of Europe and the Making of the First World War* (Princeton, NJ: Princeton University Press, 1996).

Hibberd, D. *Wilfred Owen: A New Biography* (London: Weidenfeld & Nicolson, 2002).

Hogg, I. *The Complete Machine-Gun* (London: Phoebus, 1979).

Holmes, R. *Firing Line* (London: Pimlico, 1994).

House, J. *Toward Combined Arms Warfare: A Survey of 20th-Century Tactics, Doctrine, and Organization* (Fort Leavenworth: US Army Command and General Staff College, 1950).

Huon, J. *Proud Promise: French Autoloading Rifles 1898–1979* (Cobourg: Collector Grade Publications, 1995).

Hutchinson, G. *History and Memoir of the 33rd Battalion Machine Gun Corps, and of the 19th, 98th, 100th and 248th M.G. Companies* (London: Private, 1919).

— *Machine Guns: Their History and Tactical Employment* (Uckfield: Naval & Military Press, 2004).

Jones, D. 'Imperial Russia's Forces at War', in A Millet and W Murray (eds), *Military Effectiveness*, vol. 1 (Boston: Allen & Unwin, 1988).

Jünger, E. *Storm of Steel* (London: Penguin, 2004).

Lee, J. 'Some Lessons of the Somme: The British Infantry in 1917', in B Bond (ed.), *Look to Your Front* (Staplehurst: Spellmount 1999).

Liddell Hart, B. *The Real War* (London: Faber & Faber, 1930).

— 'An International Force', *International Affairs*, 12/2 (1933), 205–23.

Lloyd George, D. *War Memoirs*, vol. 2 (London: Ivor Nicholson & Watson, 1933).

Longstaff, F and Atteridge, A. *The Book of the Machine Gun* (London: Hugh Rees, 1917).

Ludendorff, E. *My War Memories 1914–1918*, vol. 1 (London: Hutchinson, n.d.).

Lupfer, T. *The Dynamics of Doctrine: The Change in German Tactical Doctrine During the First World War* (Fort Leavenworth: US Army Command and General Staff College, Combat Studies Institute, 1981).

Luxford, J H. *With the Machine Gunners in France and Palestine* (Auckland: Whitcombe & Tombs, 1923).

McCarthy, C. *Nobody's Child: A Brief History of the Tactical Use of Vickers Machine-Guns in the British Army 1914–1918* (London: Imperial War Museum Review, 8, 1993).

Macdonald, L. *1915: The Death of Innocence* (London: Headline, 1993).

Macky, N. 'Weapon and Target', *Army Quarterly*, 33 (1937).

Maxim, H. *My Life* (London: Methuen, 1915).

Messenger, C. *Call to Arms* (London: Weidenfeld & Nicolson, 2005).

Myrvang, F. *MG34–MG42 German Universal Machineguns* (Cobourg: Collector Grade Publications, 2002).

Nelson, T. *The World's Submachine Guns* (London: Arms & Armour Press, 1963).

Nenninger, T. 'Tactical Dysfunction in the AEF, 1917–1918', *Military Affairs*, 51/4 (1987).

— 'American Military Effectiveness in the First World War', in A Millet and W Murray (eds), *Military Effectiveness*, vol. 1 (Boston: Allen & Unwin, 1988).

Noon, G. 'Treatment of Casualties', in P. Griffith (ed.), *British Fighting Methods in the Great War* (London: Cass, 1996).

Örtner, M. 'Die K.u.K. Sturmtruppe 1916–1918', in *Österreichische Militär-geschicte*, vol. 6 (Vienna: Verlagsbuchhandlung Ströhr, 1998).

— *Storm Troops: Austro-Hungarian Assault Units and Commandos in the First World War* (Vienna: Verlag Militaria, 2005).

Ramsden, J. *Don't Mention the War* (London: Abacus, 2007).

Rawling, B. *Surviving Trench Warfare* (Toronto: University of Toronto Press, 1992).

— 'Technology in Search of a Role: The Machine Gun and the CEF in the First World War', *Material History Review* (Fall 1995).

Rinaldi, R. *The US Army in World War 1: Orders of Battle* (Newport Beach: Tiger Lily Publications, 2005).

Russell, A. *With the Machine Gun Corps from Grantham to Cologne* (London: Dranes, 1923).

— *The Machine Gunner* (Kineton: Roundwood Press, 1977).

Schindler, J. *Isonzo: The Forgotten Sacrifice of the Great War* (Westport, CT: Praeger, 2001).

Schreiber, S. *Shock Army of the British Empire* (Westport, CT: Praeger, 1997).

Sengewitz, L. 'Steyr-Armeepistole M12/P16', *Deutsche Waffen-Journal*, 6 (June 1980).

Sheffield, G. *Forgotten Victory: The First World War. Myths and Realities* (London: Review, 2002).

Showalter, D. *Tannenberg: Clash of Empires* (Hamden: Archon, 1991).

Skennerton, I. *Australian Service Machineguns* (Margate: Skennerton, 1989).

Smither, R. 'A Wonderful Idea of Fighting: The Question of Fakes in the Battle of the Somme', *Imperial War Museum Review*, 3 (1988).

Steel, N and Hart, P. *Passchendaele: The Sacrificial Ground* (London: Cassel, 2000).

Störz , D. *Rifle and Carbine 98* (Vienna: Verlag Militaria, 2006).

Strachan, H. *The First World War*, vol. 1, *To Arms* (Oxford: OUP, 2001).

Taylor, A. *The First World War: An Illustrated History* (London: Penguin, 1978).

Terraine, J (ed.). *General Jack's Diary* (London: Cassell, 2003).

— *The Smoke and the Fire* (London: Sidgwick & Jackson, 1981).

Todman, D. *The Great War: Myth and Memory* (London: Hambledon, 2005).

Travers, T. *The Killing Ground* (London: Allen & Unwin, 1987).

— 'The Evolution of British Strategy and Tactics on the Western Front in 1918: GHQ, Manpower and Technology', *Journal of Modern History*, 54/2 (1990).

Vance, J. 'Tangible Demonstrations of a Great Victory: War Trophies in Canada', *Material History Review*, 42 (1995).

Wade, E. 'From Maxim to Vickers', *Army Quarterly*, 28 (1934).

Walleghem, A van. *De oorlog te Dickebusch en omstreken 1914–1918: Derde Deel* (Bruges: Genootschap voor Geschiedenis, 1967).

Walsh, M. *CRW Nevinson: This Cult of Violence* (New Haven: Yale University Press, 2002).

Walter, J. *Central Powers Small Arms of World War One* (Marlborough: Crowood, 1989).

Winter, D. *Death's Men* (London: Penguin, 1979).

Winter, J. *The Great War in History* (Cambridge: CUP, 2005).

Wolff, L. *Das Königlich Sächsische Infanterie Regiment 'Kronprinz' Nr 104*, 3 vols (Dresden: von Baensch, 1926–8).

Wolff, L. *In Flanders Fields* (London: Longman's, Green & Co, 1959).

Wright, R. 'Machine Gun Tactics and Organization', *Army Quarterly*, 1 (1921).

Wynne, G. *If Germany Attacks: The Battle in Depth in the West* (London: Faber, 1940).

Web Sources

http://pageperso.aol.fr/mitraille123/index.htm (*Les mitrailleuses du premier conflit mondial*), Accessed Sept. 2008.

http://world.guns.ru/assault/as86-e.htm (Fedorov Avtomat), accessed Sept. 2008.

http://www.unsw.adfa.edu.au/~rmallett/Thesis/index.html (R Mallett, 'The Interplay between Technology, Tactics and Organisation in the First AIF', MA thesis, Australian Defence Force Academy, 1999), accessed Sept. 2008.

Index